Creating 6-Trait Revisers and Editors for Grade 7

30 Revision and Editing Lessons

Vicki Spandel

Writer in Residence, Great Source Education Group

PEARSON

Boston   New York   San Francisco
Mexico City   Montreal   Toronto   London   Madrid   Munich   Paris
Hong Kong   Singapore   Tokyo   Cape Town   Sydney

Thank you to the following individuals for reviewing this book.

Donna C. Horton, Hillcrest Middle School
Katherine Lukaszewicz, Booker T. Washington Middle School
Laura Stoner, Hampton Roads Academy

Executive Editor: Aurora Martínez Ramos
Editorial Assistant: Kara Kikel
Executive Marketing Manager: Krista Clark
Marketing Manager: Danae April
Production Editor: Janet Domingo
Editorial-Production Service: Kathy Smith
Composition Buyer: Linda Cox
Manufacturing Buyer: Megan Cochran
Interior Design and Composition: Schneck-DePippo Graphics
Cover Administrator: Linda Knowles

For related titles and support materials, visit our online catalog at www.allynbaconmerrill.com.

Between the time website information is gathered and then published, it is not unusual for some sites to have closed. Also, the transcription of URLs can result in typographical errors. The publisher would appreciate notification where these errors occur so that they may be corrected in subsequent editions.

ISBN-13: 978-0-205-58098-9   ISBN-10: 0-205-58098-X

Printed in the United States of America
10 9 8 7 6 5 4 3 2 1   Bind-Rite 12 11 10 09 08

**Allyn & Bacon
is an imprint of**

www.allynbaconmerrill.com

Contents

Creating Revisers and Editors

Welcome!

. . . to a series of revision and editing lessons that challenge students to be daring and confident revisers.

These lessons complement and extend instructional ideas found in my book *Creating Writers Through 6-Trait Assessment and Instruction* (for grades 3 through college). In this set of lessons—as suggested in my book—students practice revision and editing skills on text that is *not their own*, and then extend what they have learned by applying those same strategies to their own writing.

Unlike other writing and revising lessons, this set of lessons shows revision *in action*. It allows students to see drafts in process, observe exactly what a thoughtful reviser does, and compare these revisions to their own revision of the very same text. Students work individually, with partners, and in groups, and have multiple chances to experience success.

> **Please note that these lessons are a perfect complement to your own instruction or any materials, such as the *Write Traits Classroom Kits* (by Vicki Spandel and Jeff Hicks), that you may use to teach *ideas, organization, voice, word choice, sentence fluency,* and *conventions*.**

Why do we need to teach revision differently?

Traditionally, we have not really *taught* revision at all. We have only *assigned* it: "Revise this for Monday." Students who do not understand revision or who have not learned specific strategies to apply often wind up writing a longer draft, making it neater, or correcting conventional errors. This is not true revision. Revising is re-seeing, re-thinking text, and making internal changes that affect message, voice, and readability.

The six traits make it possible for us to actually *teach* revision. In order to do so effectively, however, we have to make revision visible. This starts with providing rubrics and checklists that clarify expectations. But this is *not enough*. We must show students what revision looks like, by taking a rough draft and marking it up with arrows, carets, delete symbols, and new text. The lessons in this book do three things:

They extend students' practice. Most students practice revision and editing only on their own work. Because very few of them write and revise every day, such an approach does not offer enough practice to ensure growth in skills and deepened understanding. By working on the text of other writers, students learn strategies they can apply to their own work. Not only does their writing improve, but students become significantly more efficient, confident revisers.

They show students what revision looks like. Many teachers are uncomfortable writing with or in front of students, feel they do not have time to write, or are unsure about what modeling looks like, and so they do not attempt it. As a result, most students have never seen what other writers actually *do* when they write or revise. In addition, much of the writing students do is on computer or via text messaging. The revision is either invisible (once a change is made, the history of the change is gone) or nonexistent! In these lessons, the original text remains in place, with changes superimposed so students can track what is happening.

They make revision manageable. As students move into middle grades and beyond, their writing tends to get longer, and the idea of tackling revision on a two-, three-, or five-page document, especially when they must deal with everything at once, overwhelms many of them. With this set of lessons, students work on *smaller* text, and focus on one problem (or a small handful of problems) at a time. This gives them confidence to take on something bigger.

What if I have never worked with the traits before?

One glance through this book will assure you that these are pick-up-and-go lessons. You will find this revision and editing practice *very* student and teacher friendly, even if you are new to the traits.

At the same time, I urge you to use these lessons in conjunction with the book *Creating Writers*, Fifth Edition (2009, Pearson Education). These lessons are an extension of ideas put forth in that text. The book offers *numerous* additional writing samples along with instructional strategies to help you to understand:

- What the six traits are.
- How they influence written text.
- How to use trait language in coaching your student writers.

Simply put, the traits are qualities or characteristics that define good writing. Following are definitions you can share with parents, if you wish:

The 6 Traits in a Nutshell

Trait 1

Ideas

Ideas are the heart of the message: the writer's main point or storyline, together with all the details that help make it clear and vivid for the reader.

Trait 2

Organization

Organization is the overall design or structure of the writing, including the lead (or beginning), the flow of ideas, the transitions connecting those ideas, and the conclusion (ending).

Trait 3

Voice

Voice is the writer's unique way of expressing ideas—the general sound and tone of the piece, the writer's presence in the text, the link between writer and reader, the verbal fingerprints of the writer on the page.

Trait 4

Word Choice

Word choice includes all the individual words, phrases, and expressions a writer uses to convey ideas and feelings.

Trait 5

Sentence Fluency

Sentence fluency is the flow and rhythm of the language, all the variations in sentence length and structure, and the degree to which text can be read easily and with expression.

Trait 6

Conventions

Conventions involve anything a copy editor would consider in making text easier to process, including (but not limited to) spelling, punctuation, grammar and usage, capitalization, paragraphing, spacing, and presentation on the page.

How are the lessons organized?

General Overview

In this collection, you will find **30 lessons** in all, **15 revision** lessons and **15 editing** lessons. They are alternated so that students practice revision, then editing, then revision again, and so on. Revision lessons are based on the five traits of *ideas, organization, voice, word choice*, and *sentence fluency*. Editing lessons are based on the trait of *conventions*.

Each **revision lesson** is designed to be completed within roughly **50 minutes**. Each **editing lesson** is designed to be completed within about **35–40 minutes**.

Revision lessons emphasize:

- Understanding of a foundational revision strategy
- Connection to literature
- A chance to see the strategy modeled (by the teacher)
- Collaboration between students
- Discussion, brainstorming, and sharing of ideas

Editing lessons emphasize:

- Direct instruction on one editorial concern
- Repeated practice on that editorial problem
- An opportunity to apply editorial skills

For writers who need extra time or practice . . .
All lessons in this set are designed for use with seventh grade writers and revisers. If you find a lesson is difficult for some students, you can adjust the amount of revising they do (e.g., making *a few small revisions* rather than dealing with the whole text). You can also break a revision lesson into two or three parts. Also remind students to read everything aloud as they go, and encourage students to work with partners *throughout the lesson.*

Connection to personal writing . . .
In all cases, the intent is that students move from the lesson to working on their own writing, applying the same revision or editing skills.

Specific Lesson Format and Timelines

For Revision Lessons

Preparing for a Revision Lesson To prepare, *read through the entire lesson.* Make any copies or overhead transparencies you need. Note that the format is the same for each lesson in the set. Once you are familiar with this format, the lesson flow is very easy, but of course, you should personalize each lesson *in any way you wish.*

Introducing a Revision Lesson Each revision lesson begins with (1) a short introduction describing the focus of the lesson and offering a relevant warm-up, and (2) a brief sample from literature or professional writing to help you illustrate an important writing feature: e.g., *revising by showing.*

Texts for individual lessons are short

The text for each revision lesson is deliberately kept short in order to make the lesson manageable for you. It is *not* intended to be fully representative of longer reports or essays your students may be writing. Unless otherwise directed, you should think of each sample as an *excerpt* from a potentially longer piece.

Teaching a Revision Lesson (with timelines) Revision lessons are designed to take about **50 minutes** (times will vary, depending on how much revising students do). Once you finish the Lesson Introduction, you have three options:

1. Do the lesson **all at once**

2. Divide the lesson into **two parts**

3. Divide the lesson into **three parts**

Regardless of which option you choose, the general flow goes like this:

Part 1

- Share Samples A and B.
- Discuss strengths and problems, and ask students what they might do to revise the *weaker* sample (**6–8 minutes**).
- *Optional:* Share and discuss our *suggested revision of the weaker sample* (**3 minutes**).

If you wish to divide the lesson into <u>3 parts</u>, pause here.

Part 2

- Share Sample C (*Whole Class Revision*).
- Read Sample C aloud as students follow along OR ask a student to read it aloud (**1 minute**).
- Invite students to work with a partner in identifying problems with Sample C, and to make notes they can use to coach you as you model revision of this sample (**6 minutes**).
- Invite students (as a class) to coach you as you model revision of Sample C (**6–8 minutes**). Read your revision aloud to close this portion of the lesson.
- *Optional:* Compare your whole class revision of Sample C with the suggested revision (**3 minutes**).

> **If you wish to divide the lesson into <u>2 parts</u>, pause here.**
>
> **If you are dividing the lesson into <u>3 parts</u>, pause here for the second time.**

Part 3

- Share Sample D (*Revising with Partners*).
- Ask students to revise Sample D independently, following the same strategies they used as a group for Sample C. Then, ask them to check with partners to compare strategies and results (**10–12 minutes**).
- Ask two or three pairs of students to share their revisions. The goal is to *hear some variations*, despite use of parallel strategies (**3–4 minutes**).
- *Optional:* Compare your revisions to our suggested revision of Sample D (**3 minutes**).

> **How much revision should students do?**
> The suggested revisions for *all* problematic pieces are provided to facilitate discussion and to give you models that show *possibilities*. Your revisions do not EVER need to match ours, and do not need to be as expansive as ours. Some students will revise *extensively*; beginners may do much less.

For Editing Lessons

Each **editing lesson** contains these basic components:

- Introduction and explanation of the focus skill for that lesson
- Illustrations you can share with students

- Instructions to guide you step by step through the lesson
- A sample for editing practice
- Edited copy that you can use as a model (for comparison) once students have finished their own editing

Teaching an editing lesson (with timelines) Allow about **35–40 minutes** for each editing lesson. Following is a brief estimate of how long each component is likely to take:

- Introduce the focus for the lesson (**3–4 minutes**).
- Share illustrations (**5–6 minutes**).
- Share the Editing Practice sample with students.
- Ask students to edit individually (**10–12 minutes**).
- Invite students to compare their editing with that of a partner (**3–5 minutes**).
- Invite students (as a class) to coach you as you model editing of the text (**5–6 minutes**). Read your edited copy aloud (**2 minutes**).
- Check your editing against the copy provided (**3 minutes**).

An editing checklist . . .
is provided with Lesson 30. You should feel free to share this check-list at any time during your use of these lessons. However, it may be challenging for students to apply the checklist until certain elements have been taught.

What if our changes do not agree with the suggested text?

In most cases, your editing should agree *very* closely with the copy provided. Admittedly, however, even widely used handbooks do not all agree on such issues as use of apostrophes in plurals. My suggestion is to choose one handbook that will be *your* final authority, and in the case of any disagreement, consult that handbook. In most cases, issues within editing lessons are noncontroversial, and disagreement should be minimal. (The resource texts for this set of lessons are *The Chicago Manual of Style*, 14th edition. 1993. Chicago: University of Chicago Press; and *Write Source: New Generation* (2005). Wilmington, MA: Great Source Education Group. If possible, make the latter text available to student editors during lessons.)

With revision lessons, of course, there are no "correct" answers. What matters is that you and your students identify problems in the text and revise them in a way that makes the draft clear and readable. The suggested revisions are provided *to guide you*, to make you aware of possibilities, and also to make you more comfortable discussing samples or modeling revision. They are not meant to restrict what you can or should do as writers and revisers.

Do these lessons fit well into a writing workshop?

Absolutely! Usually, a writing workshop offers a combination of direct instruction, coaching, writing and revising, and sharing. These lessons provide excellent opportunities for direct instruction and coaching, while allowing students the support of working in pairs or teams, as well as connecting reading and writing. Because they are designed to help students become independent editors and revisers, with a strong grasp of writers' vocabulary, these lessons fit very well into any writing workshop that encourages students to take charge of their own writing process. They are *not* meant to take the place of students' independent writing. Rather, they serve as a stepping stone *into* that writing—giving students just the strategies they need to take their rough drafts closer to a publishable product.

What can I do to make these lessons more effective?

Many things. Here are 15 suggestions—

- **Read *Creating Writers Through 6-Trait Assessment and Revision*,** Fifth Edition (2009. Boston: Pearson Education), for teachers working with students at grades 3 through college, and keep a copy handy to refer to as you use these lessons.

- **Make sure students have access to handbooks** (e.g., *Write Source: The New Generation,* published by Great Source Education), dictionaries, and thesauruses. Provide space on which to post a traits checklist or other lists and charts used throughout the lessons. (You will need to make your own enlarged copies.)

- At any time you feel it is appropriate during your presentation of these revision lessons, **provide students with copies of the Student 6-Point Writing Guide.** Also provide copies of the **Student Checklist** (both appear at the end of this Introduction). Students can use the **Writing Guide** and/or **Checklist** to assess their own writing *prior to revision.*

- Encourage students to **keep writing folders.** Any drafts they put into those folders can be assessed and revised, then edited, using skills they develop through these lessons.

- **Do not assess *everything*** students create. It will be overwhelming for both them and you. Also, do not evaluate the work they do in conjunction with these lessons except in the sense that they *complete* all revision and editing activities. Think of the lessons as rehearsal for revision of any rough drafts they may have in their writing folders.

- **Allow extended writing time.** Encourage students to occasionally choose a draft of their own work to revise, applying strategies learned from this lesson set. Recognize that both writing and revising are reflective activities that require time, some of which should be provided during class, where student writers have access to resources and to coaching from peers and from you.

- **When students have written a draft, let them "abandon" it mentally for a time** by putting it into the writing folder, and doing nothing more with it for three or more days. During this time, present one or more revision/editing lessons. When students return to their drafts, they will see their writing with fresh eyes, and will have in their minds specific skills to apply as they revise. The difference will impress you—and encourage them.

- **Remind students to double space rough drafts**, and to leave large side margins, providing room for revision and editorial notes. Even if they work on computers, encourage them to format drafts in this way. That way, they can make notes on printed copy to guide the revision they later do electronically.

- **Keep revision small and focused**. Changing one sentence or inserting one or two details is a good beginning for some students. Encourage experimentation. Do not expect most of your students to do as much revision as you will see in our examples. Those are provided for discussion purposes to help you and your students see various possibilities. There is *no expectation* that any one student will make *every possible revision*.

- **Adapt lessons for challenged writers**. Because the lessons focus on one aspect of revision, they are already fairly manageable in scope. But you can make them simpler still by (1) asking students who are having difficulty to make only *one* small change, rather than focusing on a full paragraph or page; (2) ensuring that any student who is struggling has a partner with whom to work, even during those times when other students may be working independently; (3) encouraging struggling students to talk through their ideas for revision before putting anything on paper; and (4) using the recommended literature to provide models (sentences, words, phrases, images, details) that students can refer to or even copy verbatim.

- **Challenge those writers who are ready**. Every lesson concludes with a section called "Next Steps," which includes suggestions for writers who need "an additional challenge." Students who need a challenge should also routinely do more than one round of revision on a single draft. Professional writers do numerous revisions of important documents and manuscripts. Many seventh graders are ready for multiple revisions, doing round one and then putting the draft away for a day or more before tackling round two.

- **Seat students in a way that makes working in pairs (or larger teams) easy and comfortable**. Every lesson in this set encourages collaboration through discussion, oral reading, conferring, brainstorming, and assessing.

- **Write with your students**, modeling the kinds of things you would like them to do, such as double spacing copy, adding detail, changing an ending, starting sentences differently, playing with the voice, or inserting a word or phrase you like better than your original.

- **Share additional examples from good literature** with your students. One brief example is provided in each lesson, but if you can provide more examples from that and other recommended texts, you make the use of literary mentors far more powerful.

- **Make yourself as comfortable as possible with the modeling process**. You will have a suggested revision to review in advance, and you can use that suggestion to guide students' responses. However, your final draft need not look like ours. Feel free to be inventive, and to encourage creativity in your students. What matters is for them to see the revision unfold.

- **Help students understand that the kind of revision they do within these lessons is** *a beginning*. The author of a published book might revise a manuscript fifteen times—or more. The purpose of these lessons is not to create publishable drafts. The purpose is to practice *revision and editing strategies*. On their own, your students will *eventually* go much further than the lessons suggest, and will combine many strategies in revising a given document.

> **Have fun watching your students' revision and editing skills grow!**

Checklists

Creating Revisers and Editors, Grade 7

Note to the Teacher

Following is a series of checklists intended for use with this set of lessons. Use the checklists one at a time, as you are teaching the lessons for a particular trait—or pass them all out at once. It's your choice. Here are a few things to keep in mind . . .

Encourage honesty! Good writers make *numerous changes* to their text. So in filling out a checklist, the object is not to show how *perfect* your writing is, but to be such a good reader (of your own work) that you know precisely what it is within your draft that most needs attention. Remind students that most early drafts—even those written by professionals—would *not* meet all the criteria listed here.

Keep revision manageable. Once students have more than one checklist going, it is a good idea to think about how many things the writer wants to take on at once. Addressing one or two writer's problems thoroughly can improve a draft measurably. This may be sufficient for struggling writers. Many seventh graders are ready for a challenge, however, and may wish to try doing more than one revision of a given draft. For them, the lessons should be cumulative, so that they address an ever-increasing number of concerns at a time when revising their own work.

A Writing Guide is different from a checklist. A writing guide includes *numbers*, and shows a writer where his or her writing falls along a continuum of performance from beginning levels up to strong and proficient. A *6-Trait Writing Guide* (which students can use to score their own or others' writing) is provided with these lessons. It corresponds to the guide found in *Creating Writers,* Fifth Edition. Keep in mind, though, that the purpose of these lessons is to create *revisers*, not *critics*. The discussion that comes out of assessing a piece of work and talking about it with others is extremely helpful in giving writers the insight they need to write better. Scores per se are less important than the discussion itself.

A checklist, by contrast, includes no scores; it is intended as a guide to revision, a series of reminders. Like a Writing Guide, it is designed to encourage stronger writing by opening students' eyes to revision possibilities.

Organization

—— A strong lead invites you in

—— A strong ending wraps things up

—— Every detail seems to fall in the right place

—— My organization guides readers like a good road map

—— It's not *too* predictable—it includes some surprises

—— I show how ideas connect

—— The pacing is just right—not too fast or too slow

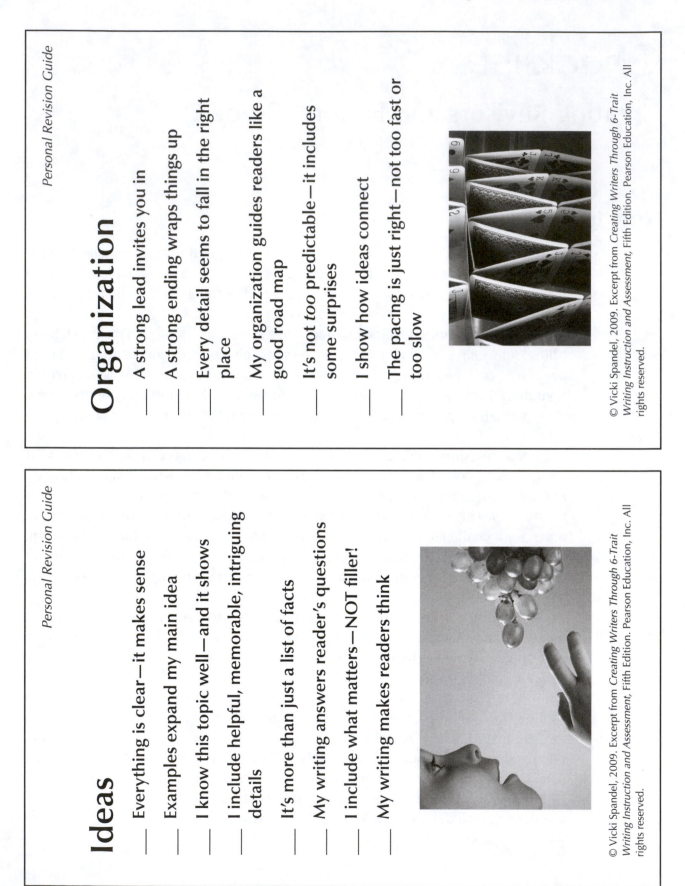

Ideas

—— Everything is clear—it makes sense

—— Examples expand my main idea

—— I know this topic well—and it shows

—— I include helpful, memorable, intriguing details

—— It's more than just a list of facts

—— My writing answers reader's questions

—— I include what matters—NOT filler!

—— My writing makes readers think

Word Choice

___ Every word and expression is "just right" for the moment

___ The writing is original and creative—I say things *my own way*

___ Words are used accurately

___ New or technical words are defined

___ The writing makes vivid pictures, movies in the reader's mind

___ Lively verbs put things into motion

___ Adjectives and adverbs aren't *overused*

___ Every word counts—I didn't use 20 words when 10 would do

Voice

___ It's individual—my fingerprints are on *every page*

___ The writing is expressive—you can tell I like this topic

___ The tone and language create the right mood

___ My knowledge of the topic gives the writing conviction

___ This piece speaks to readers

___ You'll enjoy reading it aloud

___ This is the right voice for the genre and purpose

Please note . . .

No checklist is included for Conventions because it appears in conjunction with the editing lessons.

Personal Revision Guide

Sentence Fluency

___ This writing is easy and fun to read aloud—*with expression*

___ Some sentences are long, some short

___ Sentences begin in different ways

___ Many sentence beginnings link ideas with transitions like . . . *After a while, Nevertheless, Moreover, For example, On the other hand, The next day . . .*

___ I used fragments or repetition only *for emphasis*

___ Dialogue (if used) sounds authentic and natural

Student 6-Point Writing Guide, Grade 7

Ideas

6
- My writing is clear and focused—it will hold your attention.
- I know this topic inside and out.
- I help readers learn—and make them think, imagine, envision.
- Out of many possibilities, I chose the *most intriguing* details.

5
- My writing is clear and focused.
- I know a lot about this topic.
- I share information that matters—to me and to my readers.
- I include many helpful details and examples.

4
- My paper is clear and focused most of the time.
- I know this topic well enough to write about it.
- My paper has some new information and some things most people know.
- I came up with a few details and examples.

3
- I ran out of things to say. Not every part is clear, either.
- I wish I knew more about this topic!
- It was hard to come up with new information.
- I scrambled for details. I think I repeated some things.

2
- I have a topic—*sort of*—but I'm not sure what to say about it.
- I did not know enough to write about this topic.
- I made my best guesses—or just repeated things.
- I listed some ideas—but I didn't have any good details or examples.

1
- I don't have a real topic. I'm not sure what to say.
- Without a topic, how could I have information?
- I just wrote whatever came into my head.
- I wrote what I could. It isn't really *about* anything in particular.

Organization

6
- My organization guides you right through the piece.
- My lead will hook you. My conclusion will leave you thinking.
- I link ideas in ways you might not think of on your own.
- The overall design gives a real sense of purpose to my writing.

5
- The organization helps you focus on what's most important.
- I have a strong lead and a conclusion that wraps things up.
- My transitions connect ideas clearly—you don't have to make your own connections.
- The organization makes everything easy to follow.

4
- The organization supports the ideas.
- I have a lead and conclusion. They seem OK.
- My transitions link ideas pretty clearly.
- You can follow it—but sometimes you know what's coming next.

3
- If you pay attention, you can follow my story or discussion.
- My lead and/or conclusion need some work.
- You'll need to make some connections as you read this. Or else, use the old formulas: *point one, point two, etc.*
- It's either hard to follow—or else REALLY predictable!

2
- I feel like reorganizing *everything*—beginning to end!
- My lead and conclusion are the same ones you've heard before.
- I wasn't sure how to connect these ideas. I need to think about it.
- This is very hard to follow even if you pay attention.

1
- This seems totally random—there's no pattern or design here.
- It just starts and stops. There's no lead or conclusion.
- These ideas don't really go together. They're just first thoughts.
- No one can follow this. I can't follow it myself.

Student 6-Point Writing Guide, Grade 7

Voice

6
- ☐ This is ME—as individual as my fingerprints.
- ☐ Trust me—you *will* want to share this aloud.
- ☐ I use voice to make the message resonate in your head.
- ☐ Hear the passion? I want you to love this topic as much as I do.

5
- ☐ It's original and distinctive. It will definitely stand out from the crowd.
- ☐ I think you will want to read this aloud.
- ☐ The voice fits my topic. I reach out to the audience.
- ☐ The paper is lively and expressive. I liked this topic.

4
- ☐ My writing strikes a spark or two. You *might* recognize me.
- ☐ You might share a line or two aloud.
- ☐ Though my voice fades at times, you can tell I'm thinking of the reader.
- ☐ This paper is sincere. This was an OK topic for me.

3
- ☐ My voice comes and goes. I'm not sure you could tell it's me.
- ☐ There could be a share-aloud moment or two.
- ☐ I wasn't *always* thinking of the reader. I just wrote.
- ☐ My voice is quiet in this paper.

2
- ☐ This isn't really me. It's more of an "anybody" voice.
- ☐ There could be a hint of voice in there somewhere.
- ☐ My voice is faint—just a whisper, really.
- ☐ I sound bored—or like an encyclopedia. This was NOT my topic.

1
- ☐ I'm not at home in this paper. I can't hear myself at all.
- ☐ This is definitely not a piece to share aloud.
- ☐ I couldn't get excited about the topic. You won't either.
- ☐ My voice is just—well, *missing* . . . Not even a whisper . . .

Word Choice

6
- ☐ I tried for original, creative ways to use words.
- ☐ You might read this more than once—you'll remember a phrase or two.
- ☐ Every word is important. I wouldn't cut anything.
- ☐ I used strong verbs—and precise nouns and adjectives.
- ☐ My words make vivid, memorable pictures in your mind.

5
- ☐ I wrote to make meaning clear—not to impress you.
- ☐ Once you start reading, you'll want to keep reading.
- ☐ I kept it concise.
- ☐ I used strong verbs. I didn't overdo the adjectives.
- ☐ My words help you picture things clearly.

4
- ☐ My writing is clear. I used words correctly.
- ☐ You'll notice some strong words or phrases.
- ☐ I could cut a little.
- ☐ There are some strong verbs—also vague words (*nice, fun, great*).
- ☐ My writing gives you the general picture.

3
- ☐ I used the first words that came to me—but you'll get the idea.
- ☐ Here and there is a word or phrase I like.
- ☐ It's a little cluttery. I should shorten it.
- ☐ I need more strong verbs. I might have too many adjectives.
- ☐ You'll need to use your imagination—or fill in some blanks.

2
- ☐ Watch out for tired words, vague words, or thesaurus overload!
- ☐ You'll have to look hard to find strong moments.
- ☐ It's very sketchy—or else it's so overdone the message is lost.
- ☐ Strong verbs rode into the sunset. Many words are vague or general.
- ☐ You'll have to work hard just to get the main idea.

1
- ☐ I wrote to fill space. I don't think any message comes through.
- ☐ It was a struggle to get *anything* on paper.
- ☐ I need more words, stronger words, *different* words—help!!

Student 6-Point Writing Guide, Grade 7

Sentence Fluency

6
- This is easy to read with expression and voice.
- It flows like a good song lyric or movie script.
- You won't believe the variety in my sentences.
- If I used fragments, they add punch. My dialogue is like listening in on a good conversation.

5
- You can read this with expression.
- It has a good rhythm and flow. I like the sound of it.
- My sentences begin in different ways. Some are long, some short.
- Fragments or repetition add emphasis. Dialogue sounds real.

4
- My writing sounds natural. It's easy to read aloud.
- It flows for the most part. I might smooth out a wrinkle or two.
- I have some sentence variety.
- Fragments or repetition sound OK. My dialogue is pretty natural.

3
- If you read this aloud, it's a bumpy ride. You can do it, though.
- I need to read this aloud myself and rewrite some sentences.
- I need more sentence variety.
- My fragments (if I used them) don't work. The dialogue doesn't quite sound like real people speaking.

2
- You can read this if you're patient—and you rehearse!
- I have run-ons, choppy sentences, or other sentence problems.
- My sentences are all alike—or it's hard to tell where they start.
- If I used fragments or repetition, it was by accident.

1
- This is very *hard* to read aloud, even for me.
- You need to re-read a lot—or fill in missing words as you go.
- It's hard to tell where sentences start or stop.
- I need to read this aloud, slowly. I need to rewrite sentences, finish sentences, and combine some sentences.

Conventions

6
- I edited this thoroughly. Only the pickiest editors will spot errors.
- My conventions are creative. They bring out meaning and voice.
- This paper shows off my control over many conventions.
- If layout was important, I made it appealing and eye-catching.
- This is **ready to publish.**

5
- I edited this. Errors are minor and easy to overlook.
- My conventions support the meaning and voice.
- The paper shows I know many different conventions.
- *If layout was important,* I made sure the piece had a pleasing look.
- This is ready to publish with **light touchups.**

4
- I went through it quickly. There are a few noticeable errors.
- It's very readable. The errors do not get in the way of the message.
- I have good control over basics—*end punctuation, capitals,* etc.
- *If layout was important,* I made sure it was acceptable.
- This piece needs **a good once-over** before it's published.

3
- I edited too quickly. This has noticeable, distracting errors.
- The errors could slow a reader down—or get in the way of meaning.
- Even with basics (like *easy spelling*) I had some problems.
- This needs more attention to layout (*optional*).
- This piece needs **careful, thorough editing** before it's published.

2
- Frequent, distracting errors show it's not really edited yet.
- The errors will slow a reader down—or distort the meaning.
- I made many errors, even on basics.
- I did not think too much about layout (*optional*).
- This needs **line-by-line editing** before it's published.

1
- This is not edited. There are serious, frequent errors.
- Readers will need to de-code or reread to get the meaning.
- I made many errors, even on basics like *periods* and *capitals*.
- I need to re-work the layout (*optional*).
- This needs **word-by-word editing** before it's published.

Bibliography

List of Books Referenced in Grade 7 Lesson Set

Abeel, Samantha. *My Thirteenth Winter: A Memoir*. 2003. New York: Scholastic.

Bausum, Ann. *Freedom Riders*. 2006. Washington, D. C.: National Geographic Society.

Bryson, Bill. *In a Sunburned Country*. 2001. New York: Broadway Books.

Collard, Sneed B. III. *Pocket Babies and Other Amazing Marsupials*. 2007. Plain City, OH: Darby Creek Publishing.

Donnelly, Jennifer. *A Northern Light*. 2004. New York: Harcourt.

Dowell, Frances O'Roark. *Dovey Coe*. 2000. New York: Simon and Schuster.

Dutcher, Jim and Jamie Dutcher. *Living With Wolves*. 2006. New York: Mountaineers Books.

Fleischman, Sid. *Escape! The Story of the Great Houdini*. 2006. New York: HarperCollins.

Freedman, Russell. *The Adventures of Marco Polo*. 2006. New York: Arthur A. Levine Books.

Freedman, Russell. *Who Was First? Discovering the Americas*. 2007. Boston: Houghton Mifflin.

Gantos, Jack. *Jack's Black Book*. 1997. New York: Farrar, Straus, and Giroux.

Gordon, David George. *The Compleat Cockroach*. 1996. Berkeley, CA: Ten Speed Press.

Kinney, Jeff. *Diary of a Wimpy Kid*. 2007. New York: Amulet Books.

Korman, Gordon. *No More Dead Dogs*. 2000. New York: Hyperion Books.

Kramer, Stephen. *Hidden Worlds: Looking Through a Scientist's Microscope*. 2001. Boston: Houghton Mifflin.

Kurlansky, Mark. *The Story of Salt*. 2006. New York: G. P. Putnam's Sons.

Lane, Barry and Gretchen Barnabei. *Why We Must Run With Scissors Sometimes: Voice Lessons in Persuasive Writing*. 2001. Maupin House.

LeGuin, Ursula K. *Dancing at the Edge of the World*. 1997. Grove Press.

McCammon, Robert R. *Boy's Life*. 1992. New York: Pocket Books.

Mack, Tracy. *Birdland*. 2003. New York: Scholastic.

Marrin, Albert. *Oh, Rats! The Story of Rats and People*. 2006. New York: Dutton Juvenile.

Miller, Sarah. *Miss Spitfire*. 2007. New York: Atheneum.

Montgomery, Sy. *Tree Kangaroo: An Expedition to the Cloud Forest of New Guinea*. 2006. Boston: Houghton Mifflin.

Opdyke, Irene Gut. *In My Hands: Memories of a Holocaust Rescuer*. 1999. New York: Random House.

Paulsen, Gary. *Guts*. 2001. New York: Random House.

Paulsen, Gary. *Hatchet: 20ᵗʰ Anniversary Edition*. 2007. New York: Simon and Schuster.

Schmidt, Gary D. *The Wednesday Wars*. 2007. New York: Clarion Books.

Schusterman, Neal. *The Schwa Was Here*. 2004. New York: Penguin Books.

Shelley, Mary. *Frankenstein*. 2003. New York: Barnes & Noble Classics.

Sis, Peter. *The Wall*. 2007. New York: Farrar, Straus and Giroux.

Soto, Gary. *Living Up the Street*. 1985. New York: Bantam Doubleday.

Spinelli, Jerry. *Stargirl*. 2000. New York: Alfred A. Knopf.

Thimmesh, Catherine. *Team Moon: How 400,000 People Landed Apollo 11 on the Moon*. 2006. Boston: Houghton Mifflin.

Thomas, Lewis. *The Medusa and the Snail: More Notes of a Biology Watcher*. 1995. New York: Penguin Books.

Lessons for Grade 7

Indicates editing lesson.

Revising by Showing

Trait Connection: **Ideas**

Introduction

At some time or other, most writers are told, "Show, don't tell." Great advice, all right. But what does it really *mean?* The line between showing and telling can actually be a lot more murky than those giving this advice sometimes admit. In the end, *showing* means letting a reader draw his or her own conclusions—as opposed to telling the reader directly what to think. For example, you might write, "The storm was growing dangerous." That would be *telling*. You have already drawn the conclusion for the reader—who doesn't have to figure things out for him- or herself. But let's say you write, "The rain was falling harder, loosening the earth's grip on the big maple. With each gust of wind, it tilted ever so slightly farther toward the old barn that lay in its path." That's *showing*. You are allowing the reader to decide how worried to be—but you have provided plenty of clues, along with some good imagery. And therein lies the secret to good "showing": offering just enough clues to support the conclusion you'd like your reader to draw.

Teacher's Sidebar . . .

Showing can be accomplished in several ways. The writer may paint a picture; recount an event without telling the reader how to feel about it; show a character in action, behaving in a revealing way; or disclose something about a character or an event through dialogue or internal monologue. Regardless of strategy, keep in mind that the difference between telling and showing is the difference between a mom reminding a child to wear his coat and inviting the child to step out on the porch to test the weather.

Focus and Intent

This lesson is intended to help students:

- Understand the concept of showing versus telling.
- Distinguish between writing that shows and writing that tells.
- Revise a telling passage so that it includes showing details that allow the reader to draw his or her own conclusions.

Teaching the Lesson

Step 1: Dropping Clues

Some of the following passages tell the reader what to think—and some are showing passages, offering clues that allow the reader to make his or her own decisions. Put a check (✓) beside each *showing* passage.

____ "I . . . I came in here by mistake . . . and I'm leaving." Karla did her best to stop her voice from trembling. She hid her hands behind her back so he could not see they were shaking.

____ Tyler, who was seven months old, jumped up and down in his baby swing whenever his older brother and sister played video games. He squealed as the characters bounded across the screen. His eyes grew bigger and bigger as lights flashed and colors popped. When they turned the game off, Tyler cried uncontrollably.

____ Madison felt nervous making a speech in front of the class.

____ Dylan was a daredevil. Nothing scared him.

Now take a second look. What conclusion can you draw from each showing passage? Look again at the telling passages. What information would you *remove* to turn each telling passage into a showing passage? What clues might you add?

Step 2: Making the Reading-Writing Connection

In *Dovey Coe*, heroine Dovey faces a dilemma. Her sister Caroline appears to be enamored with Parnell Caraway—but much as she wants to support her sister's wishes, Dovey herself is not so sure about Parnell. In particular, she is concerned about the way Parnell treats her younger brother Amos, who is deaf—and also highly perceptive:

Sample

I could see it in the way that Parnell could hardly bring himself to look at Amos when they passed each other in the yard or were sitting across from one another at the table. It were as though Parnell thought deafness were contagious and you could catch it just from making eye contact. Parnell never made no effort to talk to Amos, even though it was perfectly clear that Amos could read lips. The rest of us chattered away to Amos, but Parnell couldn't even bring himself to say boo.

(From *Dovey Coe* by Frances O'Roark Dowell. 2001. New York: Aladdin Paperbacks. Page 50.)

Based on this short passage, how would you describe Parnell Caraway? (Read the book to see if your impression is borne out.) Without knowing more about the characters, can you conjecture why Parnell behaves as he does toward Amos?

Step 3: Involving Students as Evaluators

Ask students to review Samples A and B, looking for indications of showing versus telling. Which author best incorporates showing details? Have students work with a partner, highlighting clues from each sample that help us to know what is really happening or how a character is thinking or feeling without the author telling us directly.

Discussing Results

Most students should find Sample B stronger. Discuss differences between the two pieces, asking students to identify specific showing or telling details from each sample. One "showing" revision of Sample A is provided.

Step 4: Modeling Revision

- Share Sample C (*Whole Class Revision*) with students. Read the original aloud—perhaps more than once.

- Talk about showing versus telling details—and underline all the telling details you identify.

- Brainstorm ways in which you could transform the telling details into showing details. Talk about how Hunter feels—and what he might do that would reveal those feelings even if we couldn't read his thoughts.

- Revise the sketch by changing telling passages to showing clues that allow the reader to make up his or her own mind. Be as inventive as you wish.

Step 5: Revising with Partners

Pass out copies of Sample D (*Revising with Partners*). Ask students to follow the basic steps you modeled with Sample C. *Working with partners,* they should:

- Read the passage aloud—more than once if that is helpful.

- Look for showing versus telling details.

- Revise by first underlining telling details—then brainstorming ways to show rather than tell (through actions, recounting of key events, or dialogue). Encourage them to discuss how the substitute teacher is feeling, and what she might do or say to let those feelings be known. Also talk about how the narrator feels, watching events unfold.

- Read the revised version aloud to see if it provides the reader with just the right clues.

Step 6: Sharing and Discussing Results

When students have finished, ask several pairs of students to share their summaries aloud. Did teams choose a range of ways to show, rather than tell? Did all revisions lead in the same general direction—or did some showing clues push readers toward a different conclusion?

Next Steps

■ Invite students to look for telling words and phrases in their own writing, and to think how they could use showing details and clues to lead a reader toward the same conclusion without stating it outright.

■ Telling is harder when you cannot use words. Invite volunteers to act out a series of emotions using gestures, hands, facial expressions, and posture or movement—then see if other students can guess what emotion is being portrayed. Volunteers might try acting *surprised, excited, puzzled, worried, irritated, bored, helpless, impatient*, etc. Talk about how volunteer actors behave to express these emotions. What do you learn that could be incorporated into writing?

■ When students share their writing in response groups, ask listeners to listen for telling or showing details—and to write them on 3x5 cards to be turned in to the writers. This provides helpful feedback for revising.

■ Watch and listen for showing details in the literature you share. Recommended:

  • *Dovey Coe* by Frances O'Roark Dowell. 2000. New York: Simon and Schuster.

  • *The Wednesday Wars* by Gary D. Schmidt. 2007. New York: Clarion Books.

  • *Miss Spitfire* by Sarah Miller. 2007. New York: Atheneum.

■ *For an additional challenge:* Telling details come largely from adjectives and descriptive labels, like *hero*. Restricting the number of these words in a passage forces the reader to show in other ways what a character, situation, or scene is like. Ask students to write an action piece, character sketch, or description that involves few or no adjectives or descriptive labels. Showing details should pop up everywhere.

Sample A: Heading Home

It was raining hard. Clouds were building in the sky. Rachel didn't mind. She liked rainy weather. She actually *enjoyed* it. Her little brother Noah felt different. He thought it might be fun to stop at the bowling alley. They could warm up there. They could even get something to eat—and bowl a line or two. Rachel thought bowling was boring. She felt like walking home in the rain—the long way.

Sample B: Wishful Thinking

Telling words?
or
Showing clues?

Each morning, Dylan walked past the Johnsons' house because there was no other way to reach the main road unless you had your own personal helicopter— something Dylan wished for on a daily basis. As soon as he got within six feet of their rather rickety wooden fence, Simba would begin his routine: *growl ominously, rush the fence, hit the wooden slats full speed, show ugly yellow teeth.*

Dylan liked to fantasize that the Johnsons were moving—to a faraway country, preferably across a very wide ocean. Some place surrounded by high mountains too dangerous to cross, or bordered by deserts in which nothing could survive.

"Just *talk* to Simba," Dylan's dad had said when Dylan explained the situation. "Talk to him in a low, soothing voice." Soothing Simba would be, Dylan thought, like trying to sooth a falling rock. Pointless, and possibly hazardous—depending on where you were standing.

Revision of Sample A: Heading Home

Rain fell in sheets.

bunched into dark fists, clenching and unclenching.

~~It was raining hard.~~ Clouds ~~were building in the sky.~~ Rachel

couldn't stop staring at all the interesting shapes they made.

~~didn't mind. She liked rainy weather~~ She actually ~~enjoyed~~

hoped for thunder and lightning.

was shivering, holding his jacket over his head.

it Her little brother Noah ~~felt different. He thought it might~~

Noah asked if they could

~~be fun to~~ stop at the bowling alley. ~~They could~~ to warm up.

"We

~~there. They~~ could even get something to eat—and bowl a

walked faster, not answering.

Wouldn't that be fun?" he asked, looking up at his sister's face.

line or two! Rachel ~~thought bowling was boring~~ She ~~felt~~

turned the corner so they would wind up

~~like~~ walking home ~~in the rain~~ the long way. Noah

splashed along beside her, trying to keep up.

Sample C: Whole Class Revision

Telling words? or Showing clues?

It was the time Hunter had been dreading since he'd come to camp three weeks ago. All the kids were going to swim from the beach to an island in the lake. The island was about half a mile away, and Hunter was positive he could not swim that far. The other kids seemed excited about it. Hunter did not feel excited at all. One of the counselors, named Sam, blew a whistle. It was time for everyone to get into the water. Hunter felt reluctant to even do this at all, and extremely worried. His feet left the sand, and he started swimming. He was pretty sure he was going to drown, and it was the scariest feeling he'd ever had in his life. About halfway across, Sam pulled alongside him in a boat. "Are you OK, buddy?" he asked Hunter. Hunter really wanted to get into that boat! Then he could feel safe.

Sample D: Revising with Partners

> Telling words?
> or
> Showing clues?

When the substitute teacher walked into the room, we could tell she was nervous. It seemed like it might be her first time teaching. You could tell she just wanted the whole day to be over with. She seemed to like reading, but she was shy.

The class did not help. They were not especially cooperative or nice. She tried hard to make friends, but we didn't let her. Later, watching her eat lunch by herself, I felt sorry for her. She looked lonely.

Suggested Revisions of C and D

Sample C: Whole Class Revision

It was the time Hunter had been dreading since he'd come to camp three weeks ago. All the kids were going to swim from the beach to an island in the lake. The island was about half a mile away, ~~and Hunter was positive he could~~ **but it might as well have been to Fiji and back.** ~~not swim that far.~~ The other kids ~~seemed excited about it~~ **were jumping up and down and pointing out to the island.** Hunter ~~did not feel excited at all.~~ **hung back behind the canoes, hoping no one would notice him.** One of the counselors, named Sam, blew a whistle. It was time for everyone to get into the water. Hunter ~~felt reluctant to even do this at all and extremely worried.~~ **eased into the lake as slowly as he could. It felt cold on his skin.** His feet left the sand, and he started swimming. ~~He was pretty sure he was going to drown, and~~ **His arms felt tired almost immediately.** ~~it was the scariest feeling he'd ever had in his life.~~ **What if he went under? Would anyone even notice? He started breathing harder.** About halfway across, Sam pulled alongside him in a boat. "Are you OK, buddy?" he asked Hunter. Hunter ~~really wanted to get into that boat! Then he could feel safe.~~ **couldn't answer. He reached for the side of the boat, and held on for dear life!**

Sample D: Revising with Partners

When the substitute teacher walked into the room, ~~we could~~ her face was pale and serious. She sat down, then stood up again like she couldn't figure out what to do. She started to take roll, then collected assignments, then got very red when we laughed. ~~tell she was nervous. It seemed like it might be her first~~ by the way she kept staring a hole through the clock that she ~~time teaching.~~ You could tell ~~she~~ just wanted the whole spent most of the class period reading aloud to us—but her voice was so soft we could barely hear her, and she skipped some parts. day to be over with. She ~~seemed to like reading, but she~~

~~was shy.~~ Kyle and Ethan talked to each other and snickered the whole time. The class did not help. ~~They were not especially~~ smiling and asking questions, but no one smiled back—or even talked to her. ~~cooperative or nice.~~ She tried ~~hard to make friends, but we~~ off in a corner, ~~didn't let her.~~ Later, watching her eat lunch by herself, I felt like a total jerk. ~~sorry for her.~~ She looked ~~lonely~~ like the last inhabitant of planet Earth, like she would die if someone didn't talk to her pretty soon.

Using Semicolons to Link Ideas

Trait Connection: **Conventions**

Introduction (Share with students in your own words—or as a handout.)

Maybe you suffer from *semicolo-phobia*, irrational fear of semicolons. OK, so we made that word up. The *fear* is real, though; it's also irrational. See? (Look back, in case that semicolon slipped by you.) As you can see for yourself, semicolons link closely related *independent clauses* (clauses that stand alone, or form a sentence). Here are some more examples (in addition to that one we just snuck in on you):

Ray forgot his comb; Bill forgot his toothbrush.

Sheila had planned to dye her hair purple; sadly, the only color left was green.

Elephants I love; it's hippos that scare me.

Any of those examples could be written as two separate sentences, with a period at the end of one and a capital to start the other. The semicolon just delivers an extra little message. It says, "These two clauses are closely connected. They go together. You should think about them together."

Another good time to use a semicolon is when the second clause starts with a word called a *coordinating conjunction*. Don't let that terminology scare you. A *coordinating conjunction* is just a word or phrase that ties ideas together, such as *however, consequently, unfortunately, moreover*, *therefore, nevertheless, for example,* and *furthermore*. Here are some examples:

Aunt Jane looked as if she would cry; <u>however</u>, she merely sniffed.

It began to grow colder; <u>furthermore</u>, the wind picked up.

Her dog Max has some bad habits; <u>for example</u>, he eats shoes.

Semicolons are also handy for separating elements in a complicated series so that we don't drown in commas. That, however, we'll save for next time. We have more than enough to do for one editing lesson.

In the text that follows, you'll find opportunities to insert six semicolons—more than enough for most editors on one small page. Inserting a semicolon is as easy as inserting a comma. Just use an editor's caret, and tuck the semicolon inside, like this:

Marcus edited 40 pages without stopping he couldn't get enough.

Teaching the Lesson (General Guidelines for Teachers)

1. Share the examples above, or make up your own examples to practice using semicolons between closely related independent clauses, or between two clauses when the second begins with a coordinating conjunction.

2. Remind students that semicolons are not *required* in place of a period and capital. They are handy, though, because they show a close relationship between the two clauses they join.

3. Share the editing lesson on the following page. Students should read the passage aloud, looking and listening for spaces where they could insert a semicolon.

4. Note that there are currently seven run-on sentences. Inserting the semicolons will take care of that problem.

5. Ask students to edit individually first, then check with a partner.

6. When everyone is done, ask them to coach you as you edit the same copy.

7. When you finish, read your edited copy aloud, explaining each semicolon by pointing out the independent clauses and the coordinating conjunctions; then compare your edited copy with our suggested text on page 35.

Editing Goal: Fill in 7 semicolons.
Follow-Up: Look for opportunities to use semicolons in your own work.

Editing Practice

Insert missing semicolons between:
- **Closely related independent clauses.**
- **Two independent clauses when the second begins with *however, consequently, moreover, therefore, unfortunately, nevertheless, for example,* or *furthermore*.**

We thought the snow would stop by midnight however, it did not. It snowed enough to blanket every roof it snowed enough to cover all but the tallest of bushes. It slowed pedestrians it stopped traffic. Snow fell right on through the night moreover, it continued during the following morning. School was delayed then it was closed. Adults wrung their hands children screamed "Hooray!" For a while it looked as if school would be closed until spring unfortunately (from the students' point of view), that was not the case.

Edited Copy

7 semicolons inserted

We thought the snow would stop by midnight; however, it

did not. It snowed enough to blanket every roof; it snowed

enough to cover all but the tallest of bushes. It slowed

pedestrians; it stopped traffic. Snow fell right on through

the night; moreover, it continued during the following

morning. School was delayed; then it was closed. Adults

wrung their hands; children screamed "Hooray!" For a

while it looked as if school would be closed until spring;

unfortunately (from the students' point of view), that was

not the case.

Revising by Making a Scene

Trait Connection: **Ideas**

Introduction

Making a *scene*—bigger than a single *image*—is a writer's opportunity to show off awareness of detail. That's because a scene comprises so many different *kinds* of detail: color, motion, shape, scents, sounds, feelings and textures, to name a few. When you think like a writer, you take in details like this all the time, knowing that sooner or later, you'll want to use the most interesting details in your writing. Think of the last time you walked through a garden or forest, sat in a kitchen, wandered through a zoo or museum, made your way down a busy street, waited in a grocery line, cheered for a sports team, watched a theater performance, or sat in traffic. If you can call up in your mind just how it looked, sounded, smelled, and felt to be in that moment, you're ready to make a scene.

Teacher's Sidebar . . .

A good scene is made up of many sensory impressions—but some always stand out. Good writers never try to capture *every* detail because in so doing, they turn a description into a list—something few readers appreciate. In planning their writing, however, they may create a sensory inventory of all the impressions their memories hold, then select those that will have the greatest impact on the reader's imagination. Questions the writer can ask in doing this are, *What stands out?* and *What makes this particular scene different from others?*

Focus and Intent

This lesson is intended to help students:

- Understand what makes for a good scene.
- Practice scene building strategies.
- Revise a scene to make it distinctive and vivid.

Teaching the Lesson

Step 1: Setting the Stage

As a class, choose a scene on which you'd like to work. Think of yourselves as staging a play that takes place in this particular setting. In creating a stage set, directors must think about creating in viewers' minds the illusion that they are right there—on the apartment rooftop, in the restaurant, at the beach, or whatever you choose. That is very similar to what a writer does in putting a reader at the scene. Possible scenes: a classroom during a test, a dugout during a playoff baseball game, an alley behind a restaurant, a street corner during rush hour, a pet shelter with people going up and down the aisles, a shopping mall during a holiday, and so on. Brainstorm a list of five or six possible sites, then choose one. Next, brainstorm all the sensory details you can think of to fill in this chart. (Keep in mind that "feelings" can include what you feel *through your skin*, or what you feel *in your heart*.)

Look over your chart carefully. What are the top five impressions—the ones not everyone would think of when first picturing this scene? Are there dominant impressions—such as a smell you can't get out of your head? Or a sound that won't stop ringing in your ears? Put stars by those. Those will form the basis of your writing. You have set the stage.

Step 2: Making the Reading-Writing Connection

In *The Wednesday Wars* by Gary D. Schmidt, seventh grader Holling Hoodhood has suffered through what most people would consider a stressful winter—one that has included, among other things, reading and taking long tests on several of Shakespeare's plays, performing in one (wearing a costume he'd just as soon forget), putting up with ridicule, battling vicious rats, enduring brutally rigorous cross country workouts, and trying to cope with the ups and downs of a family that often has little time for him. He is *more* than ready for spring break. Notice the many sensory details that help Holling set the stage for this important moment:

Sample

Spring break. Warm and green days. You know they aren't going to last, but when you start in on them, they're like a week of summer plunked down in the middle of junior high school. They mean the smell of dust and grass on a baseball diamond, the first fresh sea breezes that come all the way inland from Long Island sound, all the maples decked out in green-gold leaves. They mean checking the tennis rackets to see if winter has warped them while they hung in the garage, and watching the first rabbit running across the lawn, and neighbors putting the first "Free Kittens" signs up on their stoops.

(From *The Wednesday Wars* by Gary D. Schmidt. 2007. New York: Clarion Books. Page 199.)

Does the author put you at the scene? Do you feel you're there? Read the passage again as you look at the chart of sensory details. How many can you pull from this passage? Remember that many impressions are *suggested* in good writing, even when the writer does not state them outright. Notice that author Gary D. Schmidt is selective as he sets this "spring break" stage. He does not try to include every possible detail. Do you think he made good choices? If you were staging a scene called "Spring Break," what else might you include that is not in this passage?

Step 3: Involving Students as Evaluators

Ask students to review Samples A and B, looking and listening for sensory details that create a powerful scene. Which author stages the better scene? Have students work with a partner, highlighting sensory details that work well and thinking about others that could be added.

Discussing Results

Most students should find Sample A stronger. Discuss differences between the two pieces, asking students to identify specific sensory details from each sample. A possible revision of Sample B is provided.

Step 4: Modeling Revision

- Share Sample C (*Whole Class Revision*) with students. Read the original aloud—perhaps more than once.

- Talk about setting the stage, and ask students whether this writer has helped them to feel they are "in the moment." Identify opportunities the writer may have missed to include important details.

- Brainstorm sensory details that could be added to this scene, using a sensory detail chart.

- Revise the scene by selecting those details you feel are most powerful and telling. Remind students how important it is to be selective, and *not* to overwhelm the reader with a list of every possible sensory detail.

Step 5: Revising with Partners

Pass out copies of Sample D (*Revising with Partners*). Ask students to follow the basic steps you modeled with Sample C. *Working with partners,* they should:

- Read the passage aloud—more than once if that is helpful.

- Look and listen for sensory details that set the stage.

- Revise by first creating a sensory detail chart, then choosing a handful of details that are telling, and incorporating those into the revised draft.

- Read the revised version aloud to see if it puts the reader right at the scene.

Step 6: Sharing and Discussing Results

When students have finished, ask several pairs of students to share their revisions aloud. Did teams choose a variety of sensory details? Did the revisions sound alike—or did teams create different scenes? Which teams did the best job of putting the reader right into the moment?

Next Steps

- Create paragraphs to complete the scene for which you brainstormed sensory details in the opening activity. Read several aloud as a reminder of how many different scenes can be created for one setting—depending on what the writer chooses to emphasize.

- Invite students to strengthen scenes within their own writing by using a sensory chart to capture details buried in memory—details that do not always surface with a first draft.

- Use a sensory chart to record details from an immediate experience, such as a first snowfall, visit to a theater, camping experience, or field trip.

- When students share their writing in response groups, ask group members to listen for the single most unusual sensory detail in the piece. Record these on 3x5 cards and turn them into the writers. This feedback helps writers know which details are making the strongest impressions.

- Watch and listen for sensory details in the literature you share. Recommended:
  - *The Wednesday Wars* by Gary D. Schmidt. 2007. New York: Clarion Books.
  - *Hatchet: 20ᵗʰ Anniversary Edition* by Gary Paulsen. 2007. New York: Simon and Schuster.
  - *The Schwa Was Here* by Neal Shusterman. 2004. New York: Penguin Books.

- *For an additional challenge:* Scene making is often associated with narrative and descriptive writing. But the technique is often used to kick off an informational or persuasive piece as well. Invite students who enjoy a sense of drama to try an anecdotal lead for such a piece, creating a sense of drama by imagining that they are setting the stage for a play, and the curtain is opening on that first paragraph.

Sample A: Bus World

Wet rain gear. Boots, woolen coats, gloves, and hats. The smell filled Sarah's nostrils, mingling with the scents of grimy vinyl, a gritty floor coated in a decade's worth of old lunch crumbs, and the clumpy, unwashed hair of the two students in the seat in front of her. Sounds of laughing and yelling rose until it was hard to tell one voice from another. Sarah's feet felt hot and itchy inside her wool socks; she wished the bus driver would stop fiddling with his coffee thermos and *get going*. Sighing, she peered out the rain-streaked window at the soggy football field. Four guys were practicing, their clothes spattered so much you couldn't read their numbers. She felt a jolt as Jesse plopped himself down beside her, nudging her against the cold bus wall. "Hi," he said, flicking his black hair back with a toss of his head. "How's the football team doing?" He leaned in front of her to look out, and she could smell the mint on his breath. Jesse was a gum chewer. For just a second, the mint blocked the damp, rising odor of the bus world.

Sample B: Behind the Scenes

Sets the stage?
Sensory details?

Zach wondered what he had been thinking, taking

this job at the Sandwich Shop. He had pictured himself

waiting tables, telling hungry people about the daily

special, but he spent most of his time in the kitchen,

cleaning up. He scraped garbage off a new stack of plates,

and got them into soapy water as fast as he could. People

were rushing back and forth behind him. He could hear

them, and knew they were hurrying by. But he could not

take time to look when there was a rush. He heard someone

call his name. It was time to pick up more dirty dishes from

table 9. He dried his hands and took off.

Revision of Sample B: Behind the Scenes

Zach wondered what he had been thinking, taking this job

at the Sandwich Shop. ^(tiny, overcrowded)^ He had pictured himself waiting ^(that smelled like a big onion with a roof.)^

tables, telling hungry people about the daily special, but he

spent most of his time in the kitchen, ^(hot, steamy)^ ~~cleaning up.~~ He ^(emptying rancid grease from)^ ^(pans and fryers.)^

scraped ~~garbage off a new stack of~~ plates, and got them into ^(uneaten fish and broccoli off some chipped)^

soapy water as fast as he could. People were rushing back ^(before the steam could redden his already blistered fingers.)^

and forth behind him. ~~He could hear them, and knew~~ ^(scraping their feet over the linoleum, bumping him with their bony knees and elbows.)^

~~they were hurrying by.~~ But he could not take time to look. ^(—the garbage was overflowing with zucchini that no one ever ate.)^

^(Over the clang of banging pots and dishes, he)^ ~~when there was a rush. He~~ heard someone ~~call his name. It~~

^(yell, "Zach! Get a move on! Pick up)^ ~~was time to pick up more dirty~~ dishes from table 9!" He

dried his hands and took off ^(on his grease-stained apron)^ at a dead run, slipping in a

pool of coagulating gravy.

Sample C: Whole Class Revision

Sets the stage?
Sensory details?

If it hadn't been such an expensive baseball, Bailey wouldn't have troubled to retrieve it from where it had rolled—way, way under the front porch of Uncle Ted's fishing cabin. She crawled under slowly, keeping her hands well in front of her. Her eyes were half shut. Bailey did not really like the feeling of the earth beneath her. The smell was very strong. She squinted to see better. There it was . . . just on the other side of some debris. Three feet to go. Her fingertips reached out, brushing against several other objects before finally closing around the seams of the baseball.

Now . . . somehow she had to back up . . .

Sample D: Revising with Partners

"Who goes to the carnival grounds after the carnival is over?" That's what Micah wanted to know—but Fisher insisted they go anyway. They had to scramble over a cyclone fence to get there. The sun was just going down. Only a few tents remained, and only one of the rides was still standing. They hadn't cleaned the grounds yet. Litter was everywhere.

"It's spooky when it's this quiet," Micah whispered.

"It's *not* quiet," Fisher responded. "Shhh. *Listen.* Do you hear that?" They both listened intently, and sure enough, they could hear a noise coming from inside the tent.

Suggested Revisions of C and D

Sample C: Whole Class Revision

If it hadn't been such an expensive baseball, Bailey

wouldn't have troubled to retrieve it from where it had

rolled—way, way under the *splintery, sagging* front porch of Uncle Ted's

fishing cabin. She crawled under slowly, keeping her

hands well in front of her. *face to ward off spiders and their sticky webs.* Her eyes were half shut.

Bailey ~~did not really like~~ *recoiled at* the feeling of the *damp, spongy* earth *of decaying leaves and roots*

beneath her. The smell was very strong. She squinted to

see ~~better.~~ *in the gray light.* There it was . . . just on the other side of

some ~~debris.~~ *rotting twigs a family of slugs had staked out as their home.* Three feet to go. Her fingertips reached

out, brushing against ~~several other objects~~ *slimy leaves and mouse droppings* before

finally closing around the *hard, dry* seams of the baseball.

Now . . . somehow she had to back up . . . *she breathed in the dank air and pushed back, hoping that was moist earth beneath her hand, and not a slug.*

Sample D: Revising with Partners

"Who goes to the carnival grounds after the carnival is

over?" That's what Micah wanted to know—but Fisher

insisted they go anyway. They had to scramble over a

and the metal felt rough on their cold hands.

cyclone fence ^ to get there. The ^ *setting* sun ~~was just going down~~

lit the sky bright orange and purple.   *their canvas flaps blowing in the wind,*   *the Ferris wheel*

Only a few ^ *dark* tents remained, ^ and only ~~one of the rides~~ ^ was

like a big silver skeleton.

still standing ^ . They hadn't cleaned the grounds yet. ~~Litter~~

Flyers, candy wrappers, and old popcorn bags blew across the dust. The smell of cotton candy still lingered.

~~was everywhere~~ ^

Music drifted in from somewhere far off.

"It's spooky when it's this quiet," Micah whispered. ^

"It's *not* quiet," Fisher responded. "Shhh. *Listen.*

Do you hear that?" They both listened intently, and sure

the vigorous scratching of claws

enough, they could hear ^ ~~a noise~~ coming from ~~inside~~ ^

behind the wooden counter under

^ the tent.

Using Semicolons in a Series

Trait Connection: **Conventions**

Introduction (Share with students in your own words—or as a handout.)

Hold on, you're saying to yourself, studying the title of this lesson intently. Semicolons in a *series?* Isn't that what commas are for? Usually, yes. *Commas* in a series work like this:

> Fergus, Tanner, and Rashad all wanted to be engineers.

> Eloise grabbed her purse, climbed in the car, and headed for the sale.

The comma does series duty very well—until the elements within the series become complicated and have commas *within* them. Then, using commas to separate those elements creates confusion. There are suddenly so many commas that the reader has trouble telling where he or she is. The semicolon, on the other hand, tells the reader, "You've come to the end of one element in this series; now get ready for another." Here are two examples, expanding on the sentences you just read:

> Fergus, whose father was an engineer; Tanner, who was better at math than almost anyone in seventh grade, and liked bragging about the fact; and Rashad, who simply enjoyed building things, from tree houses to tool racks, all wanted to be engineers.

> Eloise grabbed her purse, which she was hoping still held her credit cards, money, and glasses; climbed in the car, which still held packages from her last shopping trip; and headed for the sale, where bargains beckoned to her.

If you imagine commas in place of the semicolons in those two sentences, you'll see immediately how confusing that kind of punctuation would be. Remember, the whole point of punctuation—the only reason we bother with it at all—is to tell a reader how to read and interpret what we write. To help you decide whether to use commas or semicolons to separate elements in a series, let's try a warm-up.

Warm-Up

Following are some practice sentences, each a little trickier than the last.

1. In this first sentence, use commas to separate elements in a series:

   Tarik wanted to finish the race take a shower and have a hot dinner.

2. Now let's try using semicolons to separate elements in a complex series, where each element already has commas in it. The commas are already inserted. You just have to figure out where elements one and two end, and put semicolons after them.

   My favorite seasons are fall, when the leaves turn color winter, when I can practice my favorite sport, skiing and spring, when everything is in bloom.

3. OK—now for a bit more of a challenge. The following sentence contains no commas OR semicolons. You need to fill them *all* in. Give it a try:

   Blair really loved the writing of Gary D. Schmidt who was a master at description Gary Paulsen who wrote the best adventure stories ever and Neal Shusterman who had a sense of humor that matched Blair's perfectly.

Teaching the Lesson (General Guidelines for Teachers)

1. Share the examples above, or make up your own examples to practice using semicolons to separate complex elements in a series.

2. Remind students that semicolons are only used in a series in which the individual elements *already contain commas*.

3. Complete the warm-up sentences and share answers.

4. Share the editing lesson on the following page. Students should read the passage aloud, looking and listening for items in a series, and filling in commas or semicolons.

5. They should find four series. Two of the series require only commas. Two require commas and semicolons.

6. Ask students to edit individually first, then check with a partner.

7. When everyone is done, ask them to coach you as you edit the same copy.

8. When you finish, read your edited copy aloud, explaining each comma or semicolon within each of the four series; then compare your edited copy with our suggested text on page 51.

**Editing Goal: Punctuate four series using commas and semicolons.
Follow-Up: Punctuate series correctly in your own work.**

Answers to Warm-Up

1. Tarik wanted to finish the race, take a shower, and have a hot dinner.

2. My favorite seasons are fall, when the leaves turn color; winter, when I can practice my favorite sport, skiing; and spring, when everything is in bloom.

3. Blair really loved the writing of Gary D. Schmidt, who was a master at description; Gary Paulsen, who wrote the best adventure stories ever; and Neal Shusterman, who had a sense of humor that matched Blair's perfectly.

Editing Practice

Punctuate each series in the following text, using:
- **Commas to separate simple elements.**
- **Semicolons to separate complex elements that already require commas.**

Elaina was designing a house that would be light roomy and comfortable. It would include a large great room where the television would be a cozy kitchen where the family could gather for meals and three bedrooms one for parents one for children and one for guests. The special features included a deck fireplace and large storage area. Elaina was particularly proud of the fireplace which was made of river rock the deck which ran the full length of the house and the front entry which included a skylight a large window and a mirror to capture light and make the entry even brighter.

Edited Copy

4 series punctuated using commas and semicolons

Elaina was designing a house that would be light, roomy, and comfortable. It would include a large great room, where the television would be; a cozy kitchen, where the family could gather for meals; and three bedrooms, one for parents, one for children, and one for guests. The special features included a deck, fireplace, and large storage area. Elaina was particularly proud of the fireplace, which was made of river rock; the deck, which ran the full length of the house; and the front entry, which included a skylight, a large window, and a mirror to capture light and make the entry even brighter.

Revising Beyond the List

Trait Connection: **Ideas**

Introduction

Many writers are good at hunting up information—then wind up sharing it in the form of a random list. When information comes in an avalanche of miscellaneous facts and observations, it's difficult for the reader to make sense of it, or figure out the writer's main point. A good research piece cannot just say to the reader, "Here! Have some data!" It needs to say, "I've sifted through the data for the best information—and now let me help you make sense of it." Make sure that your own writing goes beyond the "list" stage. Lists are helpful in planning writing (or shopping), but they do not make for good reading, and they do not help readers think through issues or learn new information. Whether you are creating an informational or a persuasive piece, *have a main message*. Then share what relates to that message—not *every fact* your research has uncovered.

Teacher's Sidebar . . .

In this lesson, students are given a "fact sheet," a list of random bits of information from which to build an informational or persuasive paragraph. Sources are given for the facts, and you may wish to check those sources for additional information or add data from your own knowledge or research, if you want to make the lesson more challenging. Rather than revise existing paragraphs, as in most lessons, students are asked this time to underline information central to the main message, and then build on it by adding relevant information from each fact sheet. Encourage them to consider what is relevant to the message at hand, and *not* to include everything.

Focus and Intent

This lesson is intended to help students:

- Understand the difference between a clear message and a list of random facts.
- Recognize "listy" writing.
- Revise a list posing as a paragraph so that it has substance and makes a point.

Teaching the Lesson

Step 1: Unmasking the Lists

Following are three-sentence samples, some of which are really lists masquerading as informational messages. The others actually have a point to make—and could be the start of a strong informational or persuasive piece. Read each one carefully, and put a check (✓) beside each set of statements that makes *one* clear point and offers readers a message with substance.

____ U.S. housing prices have risen fairly steadily during past decades. In recent years, however, prices have seen a sudden decline in many parts of the country. Several economic factors have contributed to this decline.

____ Lions hunt in groups, sometimes at dusk—sometimes even at night. Lions in zoos tend to live longer than lions in the wild. When a new male takes over a lion pride, it may kill the cubs fathered by another lion.

____ Humpback whales are a migratory species. A number of ocean mammals migrate, though all have different geographic patterns. Recent technology has made the study of ocean life far easier and more rewarding.

____ Though it may not necessary to be an expert in grammar, ability to speak and write correctly helps most business people succeed. Any business executive must know to craft graceful sentences, and create reports, emails, or memos in which spelling and punctuation are flawless. People in the business world are unforgiving of errors in business correspondence.

Notice that samples #2 and #3 have no center, no core meaning. Each is a random list of statements that appear to have come together quite by accident. Try this. Underline the first sentence in those two sets (#2 and #3). Then, as a class, brainstorm the *kinds* of information you would *expect* this writer to tell you next if that were the *only sentence you had read*. Compare your list to what the writer actually wrote. You should see some big differences.

Step 2: Making the Reading-Writing Connection

In his book *The Compleat Cockroach*, scientist and author David George Gordon treats readers to an abundance of unusual and intriguing facts about one of nature's most successful organisms. Gordon is an expert at grouping together those tidbits of info that go together—and omitting what is not needed. See if you can zero in on the main point of this particular passage:

Sample

A cockroach is truly the beast with two brains. It has two pairs of large nerve ganglia in its head, as well as a single nerve ganglion in its tail. These two sensory centers are connected, ultimately, by giant fibers. The components of a neural info highway, these giant fibers carry impulses ten times faster than ordinary nerves—they travel the length of a roach's nerve cord in around .003 seconds . . . The faintest breeze that precedes a rolled-up newspaper on the downswing is all it takes to give roaches a running head start.

(From *The Compleat Cockroach* by David George Gordon. 1996. Berkeley, CA: Ten Speed Press, p. 15.)

Now you know why (in case you've ever tried it) a cockroach is such a difficult creature to kill—or even to surprise. Do these sentences sound like a random list of facts—or do they come together to form one clear message? What *is* the main point of this passage?

Step 3: Involving Students as Evaluators

Ask students to review Samples A and B, looking first at the fact sheet for each piece, then asking whether the paragraph that follows is a mere list of facts and observations, or a unified message that makes a key point. Have students work with a partner, identifying the main point of each piece—or deciding that it is more of a list.

Discussing Results

Most students should find Sample B stronger. Discuss differences between the two pieces, asking students to discuss what main message Writer A might focus on, and which bits of information should be kept—and which should be trashed. A possible revision of Sample A is provided. Please note that for this revision, we have underlined what could be kept from the original draft, then built upon that to create a strong message.

Step 4: Modeling Revision

- Share Sample C (*Whole Class Revision*) with students. Give students time to look over the fact sheet. Then, read the paragraph based on those facts aloud—perhaps more than once.

- Talk about whether the writer has made the best use of the available information. First, is the paragraph a clear message with purpose and substance—or just a list? Does the writer include information that is not relevant to the point at hand—or overlook things that would support or expand the key message?

- Identify what is—or could be—the writer's main point. (There is more than one possibility; choose one.) Then, review the fact sheet as a class, identifying details you feel connect to this main point.

- Ask students to revise the paragraph by underlining what could be kept, and then building on it, drawing from the fact sheet. They may also, of course, use their personal knowledge or original research.

Step 5: Revising with Partners

Pass out copies of Sample D (*Revising with Partners*). Ask students to follow the basic steps you modeled with Sample C. *Working with partners,* they should:

- Look over the fact sheet, then read the passage aloud—looking back at the fact sheet to see what the writer has captured or omitted.

- Look and listen for a main point or thesis—the core of the writing. (Note that it is possible to identify more than one core idea, and students are free to choose the one they wish to focus on.)

- Revise by first identifying the main point, then highlighting those things from the fact sheet that support that point (four to five is a good number to shoot for).

- Create a new short paragraph that goes beyond the "list stage" to make a clear, substantive point, using information from the fact sheet as support.

Step 6: Sharing and Discussing Results

When students have finished, ask several pairs of students to share their revisions aloud. Are teams' messages similar—or different? Did they tend to use the same information from the fact sheet? Did any teams add information from their own knowledge or personal research?

Next Steps

- Choose a topic and design a class fact sheet to which each student has a chance to contribute. Ask each student to look up *one* interesting fact—and to cite the source. List the "top 10" facts (identified by class vote), and invite students to create a paragraph based on the results. Make sure each paragraph has a core—a main point or thesis.

- Discuss how the fact-sheet strategy could work when an author is drawing from multiple sources.

- Practice identifying the informational core (thesis, main idea) of any informational passage. Ask students to bring in samples to share with the class, and trade them. Talk about which writers make the core idea clear, and which do not. What techniques do successful writers use to make sure their writing is more than just a list?

- Invite students to strengthen their own informational (or persuasive) writing by doing this lesson *in reverse*. If the writing is strong, they should be able to create a fact sheet based upon it. If they cannot come up with three to four bits of key information per paragraph, they may need to do additional research.

- Watch and listen for core ideas in the nonfiction literature you share. Any good periodical, such as *National Geographic*, will provide numerous examples. Recommended texts from which to draw sample paragraphs (it is not necessary to share the whole text):

  - *The Compleat Cockroach* by David George Gordon. 1996. Berkeley, CA: Ten Speed Press.

  - *In a Sunburned Country* by Bill Bryson. 2001. New York: Broadway Books.

  - *Team Moon: How 400,000 People Landed Apollo 11 on the Moon* by Catherine Thimmesh. 2006. Boston: Houghton Mifflin.

  - *Tree Kangaroo: An Expedition to the Cloud Forest of New Guinea* by Sy Montgomery. 2006. Boston: Houghton Mifflin.

  For easier reading that is still informationally strong, try one of these:

  - *Oh, Rats! The Story of Rats and People* by Albert Marrin. 2006. New York: Dutton Juvenile.

  - *The Story of Salt* by Mark Kurlansky. 2006. New York: G. P. Putnam's Sons.

- *For an additional challenge:* This lesson focuses (for reasons of time) on single paragraphs, but obviously, most informational pieces are far longer. Invite students to work in groups, using the basic strategy of this lesson: working from a fact sheet. Ask them to create the fact sheet as a team, then divide it into mini-chapters, each with its own focus, or core. Then, ask them to write a report that is in essence a short chapter book, taking one to two chapters each. Bind the result, and share it in your school library as an example of informational writing that goes beyond the list.

Sample A

Fact Sheet*
- There are 12,000 ant species.
- Ants are found throughout the world.
- Ants are social insects.
- Ants communicate by chemicals, scents, and touch.
- Thousands of ants share one colony.
- The queen ant lives up to 20 years.
- The queen ant is the largest ant in the colony.
- Worker ants do all chores—find food, build tunnels, defend the colony.
- All worker ants are female.
- An ant chamber has one main entrance and some ventilation holes.
- Ants actually perform "spring cleaning" of their tunnels.
- Male ants mate with the queen—then die.
- Ants are omnivorous.
- They eat grain and seeds.
- Some ants migrate when food runs out.
- Major predators include lizards, frogs, woodpeckers, beetles—and chimpanzees.
- People eat ants—and feed their eggs to pets, such as fish or birds.
- Carpenter ants cause damage to buildings.
- Some ants eat harmful insects and caterpillars that damage crops.

Source: The Fascinating World of Ants by Angels Julivert. 1991. Hauppauge, NY: Barron's Educational Series, pp. 4–28.

Ants are normally considered harmful insects. They are found almost everywhere—in almost every country throughout the world. There are many different species. They eat everything, including picnic food, and the wood in humans' houses. Ants' primary predators are frogs and birds, and lizards. In some parts of the world, people eat ants. Ants are social, and live in colonies. Occasionally, if their food source runs out, they will migrate. Ants eat caterpillars—which is a help to farmers. They also eat grains, however. Some queen ants can live up to 20 years, laying enormous numbers of eggs.

Sample B

Fact Sheet*

- ❏ Australia is the sixth largest country in the world.
- ❏ It is both an island and a continent.
- ❏ About four fifths of the life forms on Australia cannot be found elsewhere.
- ❏ Much of Australia is dry, hot, and hostile to life.
- ❏ Australia is famous for the Great Barrier Reef—the largest living thing on Earth.
- ❏ Many ancient fossils have been found in Australia.
- ❏ Australia is the largest island on Earth.
- ❏ Some animals, such as the kangaroo, live only in Australia.
- ❏ Australia is home to many poisonous species, including snakes and spiders.
- ❏ Australia is also home to crocodiles.
- ❏ Aborigines are likely the first people to inhabit Australia.
- ❏ When it is summer in North America, it is winter in Australia—and vice versa.
- ❏ Captain James Cook is often given credit for discovering Australia.
- ❏ An early ancestor of the ant—*Nothomyrmecia*—has been found in Australia.
- ❏ *Nothomyrmecia* was once thought to be extinct.
- ❏ Australia is the only continent that is also a country.

**Source: In a Sunburned Country* by Bill Bryson. 2001. New York: Broadway Books, pp. 6–9.

Australia, a country, continent, and island all rolled into one, is a fascinating place, teeming with life—much of it unique. Though the land seems dry and hostile, even barren, it is actually home to countless life forms—and most of the country's species, such as the kangaroo, are found nowhere else in the world. Australia is also home to many poisonous species, including a variety of snakes and spiders. Perhaps the most famous of its landmarks is the one tourists from throughout the world come to see: the Great Barrier Reef. The reef is the largest living thing on Earth. Most tourists are less intrigued by fossils, but these ancient remnants of earlier life forms can be found in abundance as well, showing that life has flourished in Australia for eons. In fact, *Nothomyrmecia*—an ancient ancestor of the modern ant, once thought extinct—has been discovered in Australia.

Revision of Sample A: The Ant*

Note: Review the fact sheet as you look at this revision.

First Draft "List" with Core Ideas Underlined

<u>Ants are normally considered harmful insects</u>. They are found almost everywhere—in almost every country throughout the world. There are many different species. <u>They eat everything, including picnic food, and the wood in humans' houses</u>. Ants' primary predators are frogs and birds, and lizards. In some parts of the world, people eat ants. Ants are social, and live in colonies. Occasionally, if their food source runs out, they will migrate. <u>Ants eat caterpillars—which is a help to farmers. They also eat grains, however</u>. Some queen ants can live up to 20 years, laying enormous numbers of eggs.

Source: The Fascinating World of Ants by Angels Julivert. 1991. Hauppauge, NY: Barron's Educational Series, pp. 4-28.

New Version: Beyond the List

Ants are normally considered harmful insects. And no wonder. They are omnivorous, and eat everything from picnic food to grains. Carpenter ants even destroy buildings by consuming the wood. Because there are so many ants—more than 12,000 species in all—battling them is extremely difficult. They do have natural enemies, including lizards, frogs, woodpeckers, beetles—and even chimpanzees. In some cultures, ants and their eggs are used for food—but with queen ants laying eggs for up to 20 years, it would take a lot of consumption to make a difference. Another reason ants are hard to battle is that they are organized, social creatures. They communicate with one another effectively, through chemicals, scents, and even touch. They build homes that are hard to invade—and will relocate if they need to. Even if we dislike them, however, we can take comfort in the fact that they actually are beneficial sometimes. Ants eat both caterpillars and beetles that might otherwise destroy crops. So—let's hear it for the ant.

What's the core idea?

Sample C: Whole Class Revision

Fact Sheet*
- ❑ Whales were endangered during the 1960s and 1970s.
- ❑ Commercial hunting had reduced the worldwide whale population.
- ❑ Humpback whales often sing to each other.
- ❑ Humpbacks give birth in the 'Au'au Channel off the coast of Maui.
- ❑ An adult male humpback can weigh 45 tons.
- ❑ Whales are migratory.
- ❑ Babies are born during winter months.
- ❑ They journey north to Alaskan or Canadian waters to feed during summer.
- ❑ In the late 1960s, there was an international ban on killing whales.

- ❑ SPLASH is a three-year census of the world humpback whale population.
- ❑ SPLASH estimates the North Pacific humpback whale population at 10,000 to 25,000 whales.
- ❑ In the 1960s, there were only a few thousand humpback whales remaining.
- ❑ Humpbacks live primarily on krill.
- ❑ Young humpbacks gain dozens of pounds daily.
- ❑ Baby humpbacks double in size within one year.
- ❑ Humpbacks excite whale watchers by "breaching," or rising from the water.

*Source: Douglas H. Chadwick. "What are they doing down there?" *National Geographic*. January 2007. Pages 72–93.

Whales live mostly on krill—tiny shrimp-like animals. It is hard to imagine growing so big on this diet, but the male humpback whale can grow to a remarkable 45 tons. At one time, the killing of whales was legal. Whales were endangered during the 1960s and 1970s, but their population is growing. Baby whales live on their mother's milk, and gain dozens of pounds a day. After a year or so, they also eat krill. Whales are migratory, and eat most of their food in the summer. The babies are born in the winter months, many of them off the coast of Maui. Later, they travel to Alaska or Canada to eat. There are now estimated to be 10,000 to 25,000 humpback whales in the Northern Pacific Ocean. In the 1960s, there were only a few thousand humpback whales remaining. An organization called SPLASH has conducted a recent, careful census of the whale population. Whale watchers love to watch a whale breach, or rise from the water.

Core idea?

Sample D: Revising with Partners

Fact Sheet*
- The Earth is often bombarded by meteorites.
- Some are huge and potentially destructive, some no bigger than a grain of sand.
- Earth revolves on its axis every 24 hours, and this constitutes a day.
- Earth goes through natural cycles of warming and cooling.
- Some scientists believe that greenhouse gases, released by automobiles and power plants, are speeding the warming process.
- A so-called "shooting star" is actually a meteorite burning up.
- Three fourths of the Earth is covered with water.
- Air on earth is breathable—this is not true on other planets.
- Earth has drinkable water.
- It is too hot or cold on other planets to support life as we know it.
- Six other planets are visible from Earth without a telescope: Mercury, Venus, Mars, Jupiter, Saturn, and Uranus.
- From space, Earth looks mostly blue.
- Brown and green land masses are also visible.
- From space, one can see clouds over-hanging Earth.
- The whiteness of the polar ice caps is vis-ible from space.

*Source: *Next Stop Neptune: Experiencing the Solar System* by Alvin Jenkins. 2004. Boston: Houghton Mifflin, unpaginated.

Earth is part of a larger solar system with eight other planets revolving around the sun. (Pluto was once considered a planet, but no longer.) Other planets are visible from Earth, including Mercury, Venus, Mars, and others. We can also see meteorites from Earth. A shooting star is actually a meteorite burning up. If extremely large meteorites strike Earth, they can do damage. Small ones, no larger than a grain of sand, have little impact. Earth revolves on its axis every 24 hours, and this is the length of a day. From space, Earth looks different. Earth is three-fourths water. The polar caps are also white. Other planets are much hotter or colder than Earth. Earth goes through natural warming and cooling cycles. Some scientists believe greenhouse gas emissions speed the warming process.

Core idea?

Suggested Revisions of C and D

Sample C: Whole Class Revision
Note: Review the fact sheet as you look at this revision.

First Draft "List" with Core Ideas Underlined

Whales live mostly on krill—tiny shrimp-like animals. It is hard to imagine growing so big on this diet, but the male humpback whale can grow to a remarkable 45 tons. At one time, the killing of whales was legal. Whales were endangered during the 1960s and 1970s, but their population is growing. Baby whales live on their mother's milk, and gain dozens of pounds a day. After a year or so, they also eat krill. Whales are migratory, and eat most of their food in the summer. The babies are born in the winter months, many of them off the coast of Maui. Later, they travel to Alaska or Canada to eat. There are now estimated to be 10,000 to 25,000 humpback whales in the Northern Pacific Ocean. In the 1960s, there were only a few thousand humpback whales remaining. An organization called SPLASH has conducted a recent, careful census of the whale population. Whale watchers love to watch a whale breach, or rise from the water.

Source: Douglas H. Chadwick. "What are they doing down there?" *National Geographic.* January 2007. Pages 72–93.

New Version: Beyond the List

At one time, the killing of humpback whales was legal. So many were killed, in fact, that by the 1960s and 1970s, the worldwide population had dwindled to just a few thousand. Then, in the late 1960s, a worldwide ban was imposed on the killing of humpbacks. Though they remained endangered throughout the 1970s, they gradually began making a comeback. An agency known as SPLASH has recently taken a census, and estimates that the current population of humpbacks is somewhere between 10,000 and 25,000 whales—and that is just in the Northern Pacific Ocean. For whale watchers who love the thrill of watching a 45-ton animal rise right up out of the water, this is good news indeed.

What's the core idea?
What did the writer let go of to give the paragraph focus?

Sample D: Revising with Partners
Note: Review the fact sheet as you look at this revision.

Draft "List" with Core Ideas Underlined

Earth is part of a larger solar system with eight other planets revolving around the sun. (Pluto was once considered a planet, but no longer.) Other planets are visible from Earth, including Mercury, Venus, Mars, and others. We can also see meteorites from Earth. A shooting star is actually a meteorite burning up. If extremely large meteorites strike Earth, they can do damage. Small ones, no larger than a grain of sand, have little impact. Earth revolves on its axis every 24 hours, and this is the length of a day. From space, Earth looks different. Earth is three-fourths water. The polar caps are also white. Other planets are much hotter or colder than Earth. Earth goes through natural warming and cooling cycles. Some scientists believe greenhouse gas emissions speed the warming process.

Source: Next Stop Neptune: Experiencing the Solar System by Alvin Jenkins. 2004. Boston: Houghton Mifflin, unpaginated.

New Version: Beyond the List

From space, Earth looks different. Because it is mostly water, it looks blue, though green and brown patches of land are also visible—and the polar ice caps are bright white. This perspective reminds us what makes Earth unique in our solar system. Of our eight planets, only Earth is inhabitable. We have breathable air. We have drinkable water. We also have moderate temperatures—not too hot or cold—that support life. Scientists who worry about global warming are concerned about keeping Earth habitable. We might enjoy watching other planets on a clear night, but the truth is, their hostile environment makes it impossible to live there. As much as we might wish to visit other planets in the solar system, we must come home to Earth—at least for now.

What's the core idea? What did the writer let go of to give the piece focus?

It's a Set-Up: Using Colons

Trait Connection: **Conventions**

Introduction (Share with students in your own words—or as a handout.)

Sometimes public speakers just stride to the podium and start right in. At other times, they are introduced—and that introduction is designed to increase interest and excitement within the audience. The colon (:) works very much the same way, drawing no attention to itself, but *a lot* of attention to what follows. A colon can be used to set up a series, key phrase, single word that carries weight, or an example (such as the one you're about to read):

Louellen was about to be arrested, and *everyone* knew the charge: murder.

Jake sought three things in life: money, love, and time to fish.

It took Betty four years, but she accomplished her goal: hiking Alaska solo.

Usually, what follows the colon is *not* a whole sentence. It *can* be, though, if the purpose is to use the introduction to set that sentence up—as in this example:

Little LeRoy had a secret: *He and he alone knew where the money was hidden.*

The "secret" sentence sets up the "money" sentence. Technically, the colon has now joined them, and they are one sentence—even though each *could* stand on its own. Notice that a *full sentence* following a colon begins with a capital.

Colons are often used after expressions such as "in this example" or "as follows." What "follows" may be a list, or an example set off from the rest of the text—like the bulleted examples in this lesson.

It is *not* appropriate to use a colon directly following a verb or between a subject and verb, as in the following *incorrect* examples:

Marge was: always late.

The bear: poked his head into our tent.

Such colons only interrupt the flow, and should be bumped out with a delete mark—or, the sentences can be reworked if the writer has a passion for colons and is just dying to use one. Notice the new "set-up" construction:

Marge's key trait was this: She was always late.

Suddenly, poking into our tent was the last thing on earth we wanted to see: a bear's head.

Did you notice the capital "s" on *She* in the first example? It's there because the colon sets up what would otherwise be a separate whole sentence: *She was always late.* In the second example, there is no capital, however, because *a bear's head* is not a sentence by itself.

Colons have other uses, too, of course. They're used in expressions of time, for example: **It was 12:17 on the dot.** They are also used following salutations in business letters—**To Whom It May Concern:** or **Dear President Brown:**

In this lesson, we will *only* be concerned with the set-up colon: the one used to introduce a series, key word, phrase, or sentence to which the writer wishes to draw special attention.

In this lesson, you'll notice that several *needed colons have been omitted.* Insert those, using a caret. Just tuck the colon inside.

In addition, several *colons are used incorrectly*, following a verb. If a colon is not needed, use a delete mark to remove it.

As always, read aloud as you edit, using the meaning and rhythm of the text to help you hear where the punctuation falls.

Teaching the Lesson (General Guidelines for Teachers)

1. Share the examples above, or make up your own examples to practice using colons to set up a series or a noteworthy word, expression, or sentence.

2. Remind students that a complete sentence set up by a colon begins with a capital letter—just as any sentence does.

3. Also remind students that colons *do not* follow verbs, and should not ever come between a subject and a verb.

4. Share the editing lesson on the following page. Students should read the passage aloud, looking and listening for (1) places to use a colon to set up what follows, and (2) places where a colon is currently used but only interrupts the sentence flow.

5. Ask students to edit individually first, then check with a partner.

6. When everyone is done, ask them to coach you as you edit the same copy.

7. When you finish, read your edited copy aloud, explaining the use or deletion of each colon; then compare your edited copy with our suggested text on page 67.

Editing Goal: Insert five needed colons. Delete four superfluous colons.
Follow-Up: Use the colon correctly in your own work.

Editing Practice

Insert needed colons.
Delete superfluous colons.

It was: a spectacular day. Spring was coming, and Shiraz

could think of only one thing racing. She was *almost* the

strongest paddler on her team; only three people could beat

her Hannah, Samantha, and Madison. They were all

outstanding because, like Shiraz, they wanted one thing

above all else to win. Trying to recall: what the coach had

taught her, Shiraz deepened her breathing, and tried to keep

it steady. Something kept bugging her, though the idea that

she might be the weak link on the team. Shaking off her

self-doubt, she: put all thoughts of losing out of her mind.

Shiraz: reminded herself what mattered on this most

important of all days she and her team had to win.

Edited Copy

5 colons inserted
4 superfluous colons deleted

It was a spectacular day. Spring was coming, and Shiraz could think of only one thing: racing. She was *almost* the strongest paddler on her team; only three people could beat her: Hannah, Samantha, and Madison. They were all outstanding because, like Shiraz, they wanted one thing above all else: to win. Trying to recall what the coach had taught her, Shiraz deepened her breathing, and tried to keep it steady. Something kept bugging her, though: the idea that she might be the weak link on the team. Shaking off her self-doubt, she put all thoughts of losing out of her mind. Shiraz reminded herself what mattered on this most important of all days: she and her team had to win.

Revising with Consequences

Trait Connection: **Organization**

Introduction

Endings are like shoes. There are many styles—and they all serve different purposes. A novel may end with a surprise twist or revelation; a poem with a wise observation or striking image; a drama with a last quip or cutting remark; an informational piece with the most striking fact the writer has up his or her sleeve. A persuasive piece is a plea to think differently or behave differently. One way to end such a piece is by reviewing the evidence, perhaps adding new weight or bringing in the voice of a trusted expert. Summary or review endings are risky, though; they can make a reader feel you are covering old ground because you are out of linguistic ammunition. Often, it works better to use the ending—the last few seconds you have with your reader—to push for change, and to clearly outline the consequences of *not* making the change you propose. To write a great persuasive ending, imagine what will happen if readers totally reject your advice or point of view. Write *that*.

Teacher's Sidebar . . .

Summary endings can be helpful and effective in highly technical or complex discussions where the reader may have difficulty following an argument or absorbing all the information in just one round. Most of the time, however, they are likely to be seen as redundant— and if the reader takes that viewpoint, the summary will kill the argument. Encourage students to think forward, and to push readers forward, examining the consequences of following the course laid out in the argument versus not following it. Keep in mind too that a consequences-based conclusion is dramatically strengthened by a good quotation from someone who agrees with the writer's point of view, and whose opinion carries weight.

Focus and Intent

This lesson is intended to help students:

- Understand the concept of "pushing for change."
- Recognize endings that spell out consequences.
- Revise a summary ending to shift the focus toward consequences.

Teaching the Lesson

Step 1: Covering Old Ground—or Pushing for New Action?

Following are four possible endings. Put a check (✓) beside each ending that pushes readers toward new action. What consequences might the writers of the summary endings invoke to spur readers into action?

____ Unless computers are made available to every student in the school, we can expect our students to fall far behind others in the state in terms of technological skill and access to research.

____ Many environmentalists object to the thinning of forests. But while we wait for them to reach a different conclusion, we place our forests—and our nearby housing developments—in ever greater danger from forest fires.

____ The debate over violence in films can be expected to continue and accelerate for many years to come. It is up to each of us to weigh the consequences for our children and for ourselves.

____ Though many people argue that consumption of soda has no effect on children, the evidence clearly suggests that it very well may influence behavior, dental health, and weight. Continued research is our best hope for understanding the impact of sugar on our children's well being.

Step 2: Making the Reading-Writing Connection

In an essay called "Showdown at Victoria Falls" (*National Geographic*, January 2007, p. 22), author Karen E. Lange outlines plans to build two hotels, 400 villas, and a golf course in an undeveloped part of Zambia's Mosi-Oa-Tunya National Park. The essay explains that the site is not only a "crucial elephant crossing," but also the only spot along this stretch of the Zambezi River that park visitors can enjoy without paying a fee. Lange wraps up her essay with a strong statement and a powerful quotation:

Sample

[Area residents] hope grassroots pressure and a legal challenge will save the park's last riverfront open space. "Even 30 years ago Victoria Falls was overdeveloped," says Ian Manning, a former park warden. "This would be a disaster."

According to Lange, what are the consequences of allowing development in this fragile area? Notice whom she chooses to quote. Does this person's opinion carry weight? Lange saves this quotation for the end of her argument. What if she had opened with the quotation? It would still have impact—but would it be as powerful as it is once the reader knows what is at stake?

Step 3: Involving Students as Evaluators

Ask students to review Samples A and B, looking and listening for a powerful conclusion that prompts readers to take action. Which author does a better job of laying out consequences? Which one settles for a summary? Have students work with a partner, discussing both pieces and highlighting words and phrases that define the consequences of inaction.

Discussing Results

Most students should find Sample A stronger. Discuss differences between the two pieces, asking students to consider ways of making the Sample B conclusion stronger. A possible revision of Sample B is provided.

Step 4: Modeling Revision

- Share Sample C (*Whole Class Revision*) with students. Read the original aloud.

- Ask whether this writer does a good job of pushing for change—or settles for a summary wrap-up. (Most students should say *summary wrap-up.*)

- Brainstorm ways of making the conclusion stronger. What specific consequences might the writer cite to prompt immediate action?

- Revise the piece by rewriting the conclusion. If students have different ideas, feel free to draft more than one conclusion, and vote on the most effective.

Step 5: Revising with Partners

Share Sample D (*Revising with Partners*). Ask students to follow the basic steps you modeled with Sample C. *Working with partners,* they should:

- Read the passage aloud, focusing on the conclusion.

- Talk about whether the conclusion spells out consequences for inaction, or merely sums up what the writer has already told us.

- Revise by drafting a new, stronger conclusion that pushes for change.

- Read the revised version aloud to see if it is likely to prompt action.

Step 6: Sharing and Discussing Results

When students have finished, ask several pairs of students to share their revised conclusions aloud. Which are the strongest? Which teams are most likely to get action? To what extent does the power of the conclusion depend upon the audience?

Next Steps

- Invite students to create persuasive essays on topics of their own choosing, paying particular attention to the endings, and making sure they challenge the reader to take action.

■ Collect samples of persuasive writing (such as editorials or advertisements) and rewrite the endings to make them calls for action. (If the piece already ends this way, work on making it stronger, perhaps by adding a quotation.) Talk about the impact this has.

■ When students share their persuasive writing in response groups, ask writers to hold off sharing the ending. Invite listeners to record on a 3x5 card the potential consequence(s) they feel would most strongly persuade them to take action. Share results with the writers.

■ Watch and listen for good endings in any persuasive writing you share. Look at advertisements, political essays and speeches, editorials—and essays from books. Recommended:

  • *Boy's Life* by Robert R. McCammon. 1992. New York: Pocket Books. (A wondrously captivating story that slips smoothly from supernatural to coming of age and back. It's mostly fiction, but the preface offers a delightful persuasive piece on the need to keep magic in our lives.)

  • *Dancing at the Edge of the World* by Ursula K. LeGuin. 1997. Grove Press. (The essay on train travel is not to be missed.)

  • *The Medusa and the Snail: More Notes of a Biology Watcher* by Lewis Thomas. 1995. New York: Penguin Books. (Thomas's comments on punctuation are worth sharing with students for their strong persuasive tone—and insights.)

  • *Why We Must Run With Scissors Sometimes: Voice Lessons in Persuasive Writing* by Barry Lane and Gretchen Barnabei. 2001. Maupin House.

■ *For an additional challenge:* Nearly any persuasive argument can be strengthened through the use of appropriate, thoughtfully selected quotations. Invite students to incorporate quotations from two sources into their essays. First, ask them to personally interview someone with expertise on the topic at hand. This might be someone they know and/or someone who works in your community. Second, look up "Famous Quotations" online and, searching by topic, find a quotation (or two) that lends not only support, but dramatic flair to the argument. Share some of the best quotations, and talk about the power of bringing another voice into the argument.

Sample A: We Need a Theater

Letter to the Editor

Summary wrap-up?
or Call for action?

Our town needs its own movie house. Currently, citizens must drive over 30 miles to the nearby town of Cottage Grove just to see a movie. That's a 60-mile round trip, and given the time involved and the price of gas, most people just won't bother. If we had a movie house, many people would not only go out to a movie, but get lunch or dinner too, and this would give a much needed boost to our local economy. Our Chamber of Commerce could emphasize the fact that our town, though small, offers first-rate entertainment. That would boost tourism, and put money in hotel owners' pockets. If we don't build the theater, we will not be able to compete with larger towns that offer more cultural amenities. While we dicker, prices will rise—and this small window of opportunity will be gone. We must convince the City Council to act without delay.

Sample B: Kindergarteners—Headed to High School?

Letter to the Local School Board

> Summary wrap-up?
> or Call for action?

This year's kindergarten class has increased in enrollment by more than 31 percent, placing enormous strains on the elementary school budget, and new demands on our kindergarten teachers. Next year's projected increase is even larger. The elementary school cannot provide space for a third kindergarten class, so the options are to use a portable building or to house late-day kindergarten in the new high school—where several classrooms now go unused. In a portable unit, children will be overcrowded. The heat may be insufficient to ensure their comfort and well-being. Teachers will not have space for necessary supplies and equipment. Because of the obvious problems with crowding, discomfort, and lack of storage, holding the third kindergarten class in an available high school classroom seems to be the best solution.

Revision of Sample B:
Kindergarteners Headed to High School

This year's kindergarten class has increased in enrollment by more than 31 percent, placing enormous strains on the elementary school budget, and new demands on our kindergarten teachers. Next year's projected increase is even larger. The elementary school cannot provide space for a third kindergarten class, so the options are to use a portable building or to house late-day kindergarten in the new high school—where several classrooms now go unused. In a portable unit, children will be overcrowded. The heat may be insufficient to ensure their comfort and well-being. Teachers will not have space for necessary supplies and equipment. ~~Because of the obvious problems with crowding, discomfort, and lack of storage, holding the third kindergarten class in an available high school classroom seems to be the best solution.~~ Our district is known for its high quality kindergarten. If we want to maintain that reputation, we must provide students with well-lighted, comfortable space in which teachers can do the best job possible. As District Superintendent Miles McGraw states, "If we ignore the needs of students and teachers, we cannot expect children entering first grade to be prepared."

Sample C: Whole Class Revision

Last month, several off-road bikers from our

county were injured in falls—and some of those injuries

could have been prevented. Clearly, we need a law

mandating that riders wear helmets. Many people object,

stating that helmets are unattractive. This may have been

true in 1950, but no one visiting a modern sports shop

could possibly agree. Designs are more stylish these days,

and *any* helmet is bound to be more attractive than

scratches and bruises. Opponents also argue that helmets

are too expensive. But a helmet costs much less than a visit

to the doctor or emergency room. Helmets are stylish,

affordable, and useful. Let's have a law also making them

mandatory!

> Summary wrap-up?
> or Call for action?

Sample D: Revising with Partners

Currently, our city parks offer no appropriate

space for dogs and their owners to recreate together. Dogs

must be kept on leashes, which restricts their exercise. If

they are allowed to run free, the city receives complaints

from people who are not dog lovers. Why not have a special

Dog Park just for dogs and their owners? Animal owners

will enjoy the park because it will be a place their dogs can

run free—and where they can play Frisbee or other games

with their pets. People who are less fond of dogs will love

having a more "animal-free" space where they won't be

bitten or jumped on while taking a walk or doing yoga.

Whether you own a pet right now or not, please join the

campaign for a new Dog Park. It will give dogs and their

owners room to roam and play Frisbee—and will allow

non-owners their own "people space."

Summary wrap-up? or Call for action?

Suggested Revisions of C and D

Sample C: Whole Class Revision

Last month, several off-road bikers from our county were injured in falls—and some of those injuries could have been prevented. Clearly, we need a law mandating that riders wear helmets. Many people object, stating that helmets are unattractive. This may have been true in 1950, but no one visiting a modern sports shop could possibly agree. Designs are more stylish these days, and *any* helmet is bound to be more attractive than scratches and bruises. Opponents also argue that helmets are too expensive. But a helmet costs much less than a visit to the doctor or emergency room. ~~Helmets are stylish, affordable, and useful. Let's have a law also making them mandatory!~~ If we let fashion sense get in the way of safety, we'll see the number of preventable injuries continue to rise. Consider the words of emergency room nurse David Riley: "The next biking accident victim could be someone you love." Don't let that become a prediction. Make helmets mandatory now.

Sample D: Revising with Partners

Currently, our city parks offer no appropriate space for dogs and their owners to recreate together. Dogs must be kept on leashes, which restricts their exercise. If they are allowed to run free, the city receives complaints from people who are not dog lovers. Why not have a special Dog Park just for dogs and their owners? Animal owners will enjoy the park because it will be a place their dogs can run free—and where they can play Frisbee or other games with their pets. People who are less fond of dogs will love having a more "animal-free" space where they won't be bitten or jumped on while taking a walk or doing yoga. Whether you own a pet right now or not, please join the campaign for a new Dog Park. ~~It will give dogs and their owners room to roam and play Frisbee—and will allow non-owners their own "people space."~~ If we don't act, the conflict between dog owners and non-owners will escalate as people and dogs fight for turf. More people will complain about "vicious" dogs, and more dogs will grow unhealthy because they have no room to run. Let's create a better scenario, with recreational space for everyone.

Putting It All Together
(Editing Lessons 2, 4, and 6)

Trait Connection: **Conventions**

Introduction (Share with students in your own words—or as a handout.)

In this lesson, you will have a chance to put together skills from three editing lessons. You will:

- Use semicolons to link closely related sentences: *We fished all day; we caught nothing.*

- Use semicolons to link two sentences when the second begins with a coordinating conjunction (*however, furthermore, since, but, nevertheless*, and so on): *We felt stuffed after three pizzas; nevertheless, no one could resist ice cream.*

- Use semicolons in a complex series where the individual elements already have commas within them: *Debra's favorite things were basketball, hockey, and camping; Denise liked photography, hiking, and reading; and Betty, who was always an independent thinker, liked sculpture, poetry, and travel.*

- Use colons to set up a series: **The game could only be halted by one of three events: flooding of the field, fire in the stands, or the unexplained disappearance of the coach.**

- Use colons to set up a word or expression to which you want to draw attention: **Whenever Betsy spotted her cousin, only one word came to mind: cockroach.**

- Delete semicolons or colons that only interrupt the flow of a sentence. *None* of the following colons or semicolons belong:

  - Earl: knew he would be famous one day.
  - Helen had to: agree.
  - Hawaii; is one of the most beautiful states in the nation.
  - In fact, it attracts; thousands of tourists annually.

Teaching the Lesson (General Guidelines for Teachers)

1. Begin by reviewing the various uses for a semicolon or colon that are covered in lessons 2, 4, and 6. Make sure all three are clear in students' minds, and answer any questions.

2. List some possible linking words (*coordinating conjunctions*) that may begin the second of two sentences joined by a semicolon: *however, therefore, nevertheless, moreover, still, but, so*, and so on. If you wish, post the list for a reference as students work.

3. Encourage students to review Lessons 2, 4, and 6—and to refer to them as they work on Lesson 8. Also provide handbooks, if you wish.

4. Share the editing lesson on the following page. Students should read the passage aloud, looking *and listening* for opportunities to use colons or semicolons—as well as for semicolons and colons that do not belong and should be deleted.

5. Ask them to work individually first, then check with a partner.

6. When everyone is done, ask them to coach you as you edit the same copy, making any changes you and they decide are important. When you finish, compare your edited copy to the one on page 82.

Editing Goal: Insert missing colons and semicolons. Delete those that do not belong. Follow-up: Use colons and semicolons correctly in your own work.

Editing Practice

Insert missing colons and semicolons.
Delete colons or semicolons that only interrupt sentence flow.

Rob and Eddie were excited they were downright thrilled, in fact. Rob's parents were going out of town for the weekend, and Eddie was staying over. For them, the whole weekend would be devoted to one goal finding out where the tunnel led. The tunnel: was actually a passageway heading down from the floor of Rob's dad's toolshed, but getting to it was hard for one reason you had to pry up the door in the floor using a toolbar. Rob was sure; they could get in they had already gotten in once. What worried him: was leaving things the same, so nothing looked disturbed. Eddie begged to go first into the tunnel however, once they got the door pried up, he lost his nerve. "OK, then here's how it is," Rob told him. "You can go first, in which case you're a hero you can wait here, in which case, you're the guard and I'm the leader of the expedition or you can forget the whole thing and run home, in which case, you lose your rights to explore the tunnel forever." Eddie sucked in a deep breath; and started down the ladder. He could see only one thing total darkness. Miraculously, he wasn't a bit frightened in fact, he was enjoying himself immensely; until he dropped the most important thing he was carrying his flashlight.

Edited Copy

Missing colons and semicolons inserted
Interruptive colons or semicolons deleted

Rob and Eddie were excited they were downright thrilled, in fact. Rob's

parents were going out of town for the weekend, and Eddie was staying

over. For them, the whole weekend would be devoted to one goal finding

out where the tunnel led. The tunnel was actually a passageway heading

down from the floor of Rob's dad's toolshed, but getting to it was hard for

one reason you had to pry up the door in the floor using a toolbar. Rob

was sure they could get in they had already gotten in once. What

worried him was leaving things the same, so nothing looked disturbed.

Eddie begged to go first into the tunnel however, once they got the door

pried up, he lost his nerve. "OK, then here's how it is," Rob told him.

"You can go first, in which case you're a hero you can wait here, in

which case, you're the guard and I'm the leader of the expedition or you

can forget the whole thing and run home, in which case, you lose your

rights to explore the tunnel forever." Eddie sucked in a deep breath and

started down the ladder. He could see only one thing total darkness.

Miraculously, he wasn't a bit frightened in fact, he was enjoying

himself immensely until he dropped the most important thing he was

carrying his flashlight.

Revising to Connect Ideas

Trait Connection: **Organization**

Introduction

Transitions link ideas in terms of time, space, or relationship. Here are a few examples of transitional words or expressions you may have used yourself: *however, nevertheless, furthermore, at the same time, for example, the next day, after a while, later that night, meanwhile, in the end, similarly, also, sometimes, whenever, in addition*. There are *countless* other possibilities, and in addition, whole sentences or even paragraphs sometimes work as transitions. Writers who omit transitions, or are careless about using the right connection, run the risk of being misinterpreted. For example, let's say I write, *Harry was happy about going to New Zealand. Many of his relatives lived there.* That sounds as if Harry's excited *because* he's likely to see relatives in New Zealand. But with the power of transitions, I can create a totally different meaning: *Harry was happy <u>about</u> going to New Zealand, <u>even though</u> many of his relatives lived there.* Now you know that Harry prefers *not* to bump into his relatives—but is willing to risk it for a chance to see New Zealand. Transitions are the chain links that connect ideas, giving the whole piece a strength and unity it wouldn't have otherwise.

Teacher's Sidebar . . .

Many students find it helpful to have a list of transitional words from which to draw—so long as they do not feel restricted to that list, and use it *only* to spur their own thinking. For an excellent list arranged by function, see the handbook *Write Source: The New Generation*, Great Source Education Group, 2005, pp. 592–593. Also keep in mind that transitions are more than single words (*therefore, however, next*) or even phrases (*later that day, in a while, for that reason*). They may also be whole sentences—or even paragraphs. This is why understanding the transitional concept is more important, ultimately, than *just* working from a list.

Focus and Intent

This lesson is intended to help students:

- Understand the concept of *transition*.
- Identify and interpret transitions in written text.
- Revise text by adding or changing transitions.

Teaching the Lesson

Step 1: Going Transitional

Following are some examples of text in which the transitions do not ring true. In each example, begin by highlighting the transitions. Then create new transitions between sentences or clauses to clarify meaning. Remember that a transition can be a single word, expression, sentence, or paragraph.

Riley got a new computer, although I did not hear from her for many months.

The burglar tried the door for over five minutes. Therefore, he broke in through a window.

Most of the time, Charley was a cheerful person. As a result, now and then, he felt the need to be alone whenever he could sort out his thoughts.

(Possible revisions appear at the end of the lesson.)

Step 2: Making the Reading-Writing Connection

In *Oh, Rats! The Story of Rats and People*, author Albert Marrin makes skillful use of connecting words and phrases to link together the numerous ideas and facts uncovered through his research. Without sound transitions, his elaborate collection of data might not be so easy to follow. With transitions, he forms a network that holds ideas together in patterns. Look for connecting words and phrases in this passage from the chapter titled "Pesky Rats":

Sample

Rats are most dangerous if backed into a corner. To "fight like a cornered rat" is an expression that means to fight fiercely and desperately. In trying to escape, a rat will leap at its attacker, going for the face and eyes.

If you should see a wild rat, follow my father's advice. Try to stay calm. Chances are, it is more afraid of you than you are of it. Most times, screaming at the top of your voice will scare it away. Running away works, too. As a rule, rats will not follow.

(From *Oh, Rats! The Story of Rats and People* by Albert Marrin. 2006. New York: Penguin, p. 24.)

How many connecting words and phrases did you find? If you looked carefully, you likely found more transitional expressions than in many pieces of writing, and this facility with transitions makes Marrin's writing exceptionally smooth and easy to follow. To see what a difference such expressions make, underline the following words and phrases in order; then read the passage without them: *if backed into a corner, In trying to escape, If you should see a wild rat, Chances are, Most times, too, As a rule*. When left with just the bare bones—all transitional expressions removed—a reader must make his/her own connections. That calls for more mental gymnastics than many readers are willing to go through.

Step 3: Involving Students as Evaluators

Ask students to review Samples A and B, looking and listening for strong transitions that hold ideas together. Which author does a better job of using transitions to create smooth flowing, coherent text? Which one settles for a barebones approach—or uses transitions inappropriately? Have students work with a partner, highlighting transitional words and phrases and making marginal notes to suggest alternatives for those that do not work well.

Discussing Results

Most students should find Sample B stronger. Discuss differences between the two pieces, asking students to consider ways of revising Sample A by changing or adding transitions. A possible revision of Sample A is provided.

Step 4: Modeling Revision

- Share Sample C (*Whole Class Revision*) with students. Read the original aloud.

- Ask whether this writer does a good job of using transitions to link ideas and create a smooth flow. (Most students should say *no*.)

- Highlight transitional words and phrases—and mark any opportunities to link ideas that the writer may have overlooked.

- Revise the piece by adding or changing transitions so that ideas are clearly connected and the whole piece reads smoothly. Check your final draft by reading it aloud.

Step 5: Revising with Partners

Share Sample D (*Revising with Partners*). Ask students to follow the basic steps you modeled with Sample C. *Working with partners,* they should:

- Read the passage aloud, focusing on transitions.

- Highlight existing transitions and mark spots where the writer has missed an opportunity to link ideas.

- Revise by drafting new transitions, or changing existing transitions to make the true link between ideas clear.

- Read the revised version aloud to see if it is smooth and easy to follow.

Step 6: Sharing and Discussing Results

When students have finished, ask several pairs of students to share their revised passages aloud. Which are the easiest to follow? Which teams did the best job of making the connections between ideas clear?

Next Steps

- Ask students to highlight transitional words and phrases within their own work, and to check whether those transitions work well or could be strengthened.

- Do occasional transitional "warm-ups," writing two declarative sentences on the board and asking students to find a way of linking them, using transitional expressions. Talk about the many different ways there are to link ideas.

- Watch and listen for strong transitions in any literature you share with students. Recommended:

  - *Oh, Rats! The Story of Rats and People* by Albert Marrin. 2006. New York: Penguin.

  - *Escape! The Story of the Great Houdini* by Sid Fleischman. 2006. New York: HarperCollins.

  - *Hidden Worlds: Looking Through a Scientist's Microscope* by Stephen Kramer. 2001. Boston: Houghton Mifflin.

  - *Jack's Black Book* by Jack Gantos. 1997. New York: Farrar, Straus, and Giroux.

- *For an additional challenge:* Pull a passage with strong transitions from literature, and reprint it for students, omitting all or most of the transitional words or phrases. Ask them to "fill in the blanks," linking ideas in a way they think makes sense. Then compare their ideas with the author's original. Did they make the same links? Did they come up with something more creative—or logical?

Possible Revisions for Warm-Up Sentences:

- Riley got a new computer, <u>although</u> I did not hear from her for many months.
  <u>After</u> Riley got a new computer, <u>she was so busy that</u> I did not hear from her for many months.

- The burglar tried the door for over five minutes. <u>Therefore</u>, he broke in through a window.
  <u>After</u> the burglar had tried the door for over five minutes, <u>he got</u> <u>discouraged</u> and <u>finally</u> broke in through a window.

- <u>Most of the time</u>, Charley was a cheerful person. <u>As a result, now and then</u>, he felt the need to be alone <u>whenever</u> he could sort out his thoughts.
  <u>Most of the time</u>, Charley was a cheerful person. <u>Now and then, however,</u> he felt the need to be alone <u>so that</u> he could sort out his thoughts.

Sample A: Yoga

Strong
transitions?
Opportunities
missed?

Many people use yoga as part of a fitness routine. Yoga is said to improve coordination, muscle strength, and circulation. Many athletes practice yoga. It improves balance and flexibility. It is a challenge for many people. They get better at it.

People who watch yoga but have not done it think it is easy. They find it is not. The moves require intense concentration. It takes patience to become very skilled. Experts recommend spending thirty minutes three times a week or more.

The rewards are great. People who master yoga claim they feel more fit. They sleep better. They reduce their stress.

Sample B: Ice Dams

Strong
transitions?
Opportunities
missed?

In areas of heavy snowfall, ice dams create a serious

problem. As snow falls, it builds on the roof of a

building. Heat from inside the building causes some of the

snow to melt, forming water. The water runs off the roof—

or tries to. When it reaches the edge of the roof, however,

there is no longer any heat from within the house to keep

the water in a liquid state. In the absence of heat, the water

re-freezes, forming ice. As the amount of ice on the edge of

the roof increases, it forms a dam, which then holds water

back. Over time, the dam grows bigger—and stronger. With

nowhere to go, additional melting water remains on the

roof. When it gets deep enough, it works its way

underneath the roof shingles, and right down the inside

walls of the building. Even a small amount of water can be

a decorative disaster. If the amount of water that leaks into

the building is extensive, though, it creates serious

structural damage.

Revision of Sample A: Yoga

Many people use yoga as part of a fitness routine. —for several reasons. Yoga is

said to improve coordination, muscle strength, and

circulation. In addition, many athletes practice yoga. because they claim that It improves

balance and flexibility. Although yoga It is a challenge for many people at first,

they get better at it. over time as their muscles strengthen and joints loosen up.

People who watch yoga but have not done it think it often mistakenly

is easy. They are surprised, upon trying it themselves, to find it is not. The moves require intense

concentration. Furthermore, it takes patience to become very skilled.

It also takes time. Experts recommend spending thirty minutes three times a

week or more.

The rewards are great. for all this effort however. People who master yoga

claim they feel more fit. They also sleep better. Best of all, they reduce their

stress.

Sample C: Whole Class Revision

Pearl & the Coyote

Pearl was a city dog. She had never been to the country before. It intrigued her. The smells and sounds of the swamp were irresistible. They almost cost Pearl her life.

Pearl was busy chasing a wild goose. The goose was protecting its nest. It wouldn't take off and fly—it just ran helter-skelter, and Pearl ran after it. She didn't hear or see or smell anything else.

A coyote was watching Pearl intently. It stalked her through the low grasses. Pearl did not see it. She kept her attention on the goose. She was not used to running in a swamp, and got herself stuck—badly—in muck up to her knees. Slowly, she tried to wade out, lifting each mud-caked foot.

The coyote saw his chance. He charged Pearl. Pearl's owner spotted the coyote and called out. The coyote took off.

Sample D: Revising with Partners

Strong transitions? Opportunities missed?

School Vending Machines

Some people want to fill school vending machines with health food, such as sunflower seeds, oranges, apples, dried fruit, or whole grain crackers. There are problems with this idea.

Most students like what is in the vending machines right now. They like sodas, candy bars, cookies, and regular crackers. They taste good. What's more, they're not all that nutritious.

A lot of students don't know much about health food. They might not buy it. It is more expensive than junk food, providing another reason not to buy it. The health food could sit in the vending machine a long time, growing stale.

School officials should ask students what their preferences are. It is important to have a voice.

Suggested Revisions of C and D

Sample C: Whole Class Revision

Pearl & the Coyote

Pearl was a city dog. *Because* She had never been to the country

before, ~~It intrigued her~~ the smells and sounds of the swamp

were irresistible, *and* they almost cost Pearl her life.

Pearl was busy chasing a wild goose. The goose, *in turn,* was

protecting its nest. *Consequently,* it wouldn't take off and fly—it just ran

helter-skelter, and Pearl ran after it. She (was so busy chasing the goose that she) didn't hear or see or

smell anything else.

Meanwhile, a coyote was watching Pearl intently. *As* it stalked her

through the low grasses, Pearl ~~did not see it. She~~ kept her

attention on the goose. (and as a result, she never saw the coyote at all. Since Pearl) ~~She~~ was not used to running in a

swamp, ~~and~~ *she* got herself stuck—badly—in muck up to her knees.

Slowly, she tried to wade out, lifting each mud-caked foot.

At that moment, the coyote saw his chance. *and* ~~He~~ charged Pearl. Pearl's *Fortunately,*

owner spotted the coyote (at the last minute,) and called out. The coyote took off, (before Pearl even caught a glimpse of him.)

Sample D: Revising with Partners

School Vending Machines

Some people want to fill school vending machines with

health food, such as sunflower seeds, oranges, apples,

however, several

dried fruit, or whole grain crackers. There are ^ problems

with this idea.

First of all,

^ most students like what is in the vending machines

Current products include such things as

right now. ~~They like~~ sodas, candy bars, cookies, and regular

Students like these foods because

crackers. They taste good ^; ~~What's more~~ ^ they're not all

that nutritious.

Second,

^ a lot of students don't know much about health food ^

and   *without more information about its benefits. What's more,*

~~They~~ might not buy it. ^ It is more expensive than junk food,

giving students a third   *With no one making purchases,*

~~providing another~~ reason not to buy it. ^ the health food

could sit in the vending machine a long time, growing stale.

If they really want this idea to work,

^ school officials should ask students what their

for students

preferences are. It is important to have a voice ^

in decisions that affect them.

Going for the Right Tense

Trait Connection: **Conventions**

Introduction (Share with students in your own words—or as a handout.)

By now, you know that verbs shift tenses to let readers know whether something is happening right now (*present tense*), has already happened (*past tense*), happened even before the immediate past (*past perfect*), or will happen sometime in the future (*future tense*).

> I am skiing right now. (*present*)
>
> Bob skies well. (*ongoing present*)
>
> I skied yesterday. (*past*)
>
> I had skied all day when I met Bob. (*past perfect*)
>
> I will ski next week if it snows. (*future*)

Using the right tense at the right time helps your readers stay oriented. It is jarring to be expecting one tense—and have the writer pull a quick shift on you. Take a look at the following samples, and see if you can figure out what verb form the writer should use for the **second** underlined verb. The first one is done for you:

- I <u>was skiing</u> down the hill when another skier <u>cuts</u> right in front of me!
  (Should be *cut*)

- I <u>had been waiting</u> an hour for the bus when finally it <u>comes</u>!
  (Should be _____)

- I <u>answered</u> the phone and to my surprise, <u>it is</u> my mom!
  (Should be _____)

- Her visit <u>had been</u> a surprise, but we <u>are</u> happy to see her.
  (Should be _____)

- She <u>looks</u> old enough to be my aunt, but she <u>was</u> actually my cousin.
  (Should be _____)

Teaching the Lesson (General Guidelines for Teachers)

1. Share the examples above, or make up your own examples to practice identifying verbs and verb tenses and avoiding jarring shifts.

2. Share the editing lesson on the following page. Students should read the passage aloud (*softly*), looking and listening for jarring shifts in tense.

3. Ask students to edit individually first, then check with a partner.

4. When everyone is done, ask them to coach you as you edit the same copy.

5. When you finish, read your edited copy aloud, explaining your choices; then compare your edited copy with our suggested text on page 97.

Editing Goal: Edit for verb tense.
Follow-Up: Check verb tenses in your own work.

Sample Sentences, Edited Version

- I <u>was skiing</u> down the hill when another skier <u>cut</u> right in front of me!

- I <u>had been waiting</u> an hour for the bus when finally it <u>came</u>!

- I <u>answered</u> the phone and to my surprise, it <u>was</u> my mom!

- Her visit <u>had been</u> a surprise, but we <u>were</u> happy to see her.

- She <u>looks</u> old enough to be my aunt, but she <u>is</u> actually my cousin.

Editing Practice

Check for verb tense.
Correct verbs that cause a sudden, jarring shift.

John Hubbard had been teaching seventh grade for almost a year when the local newspaper does an interview with him. He tells the reporter that he liked teaching a lot, and added that the best thing about teaching was working with students who loved books as much as he did. He names his two favorite authors: Sandra Cisneros and Gary Paulsen. He said they were his favorites since he is in middle school himself.

Mr. Hubbard currently teaches seventh grade, and said that when he is a seventh grader himself, he was not a good reader at all. A teacher turned him on to audio tapes, however, and Hubbard discovers that he had a good voice for reading aloud. This year he will ask his students to make an audio tape of a Harry Potter chapter. Next month, the students will choose the chapter they wanted. Hubbard has a particular student in mind for the role of Harry, but wasn't sure if the student will say yes. He is very shy.

Edited Copy

9 jarring verbs corrected for tense

John Hubbard had been teaching seventh grade for almost a year when

the local newspaper ~~does~~ *did* an interview with him. He ~~tells~~ *told* the reporter

that he liked teaching a lot, and added that the best thing about teaching

was working with students who loved books as much as he did. He

~~names~~ *named* his two favorite authors: Sandra Cisneros and Gary Paulsen. He

said they ~~were~~ *had been* his favorites since he ~~is~~ *was* in middle school himself.

    Mr. Hubbard currently teaches seventh grade, and said that when

he ~~is~~ *was* a seventh grader himself, he was not a good reader at all. A teacher

turned him on to audio tapes, however, and Hubbard ~~discovers~~ *discovered* that he

had a good voice for reading aloud. This year he will ask his students to

make an audio tape of a Harry Potter chapter. Next month, the students

will choose the chapter they ~~wanted~~ *want.* Hubbard has a particular student in

mind for the role of Harry, but ~~wasn't~~ *isn't* sure if the student will say yes. He

is very shy.

Revising Under Pressure

Trait Connection: **Organization**

Introduction

Suppose you were having unexpected company and wanted to make a good impression. What—*exactly*—would you do if you only had five minutes? That's how you're going to revise in this lesson. Quickly, efficiently—and with a plan. When time is limited—in a state writing assessment, for example—you may be tempted to forget all about revision, thinking that the best thing you can do is fill the time with drafting, writing new words and sentences right up until the last minute. Often, though, just a *short* time spent reflecting and revising can pay huge dividends. Revised writing is nearly *always* better. This plan asks you to focus on those two parts of the writing where readers pay the most attention: the lead and the conclusion. Then (if time permits) we'll do two more things. First, we'll cheat a bit and reach ahead into another trait bag of tricks: word choice. We'll look for one word—just *one*—to empower. Finally, we'll give the piece a title. So, take a deep breath, and let's go for it.

Teacher's Sidebar . . .

True revision takes time—and is best done after students have put their work away for several days so that they can see it with fresh eyes. Unfortunately, on-demand writing does not usually make provisions for the kind of revision we'd most like our students to do. This 5-minute plan teaches students survival strategies they can use to make writing *considerably* stronger when time is limited. Only you can know your own state or district requirements, but usually, in on-demand situations, students are allowed to do some crossing out and inserting, so long as they keep their work neat. That is our assumption here.

Focus and Intent

This lesson is intended to help students:

- Distinguish between true revision and on-demand revision.
- Make a revision plan they can implement in five minutes or less.
- Use their five-minute plan to revise a short essay.

Teaching the Lesson

Step 1: Making a Plan

For this part of the lesson, gather three to five of your students' favorite books, essays, or stories, and read just the lead, then just the conclusion—and finally the title. Talk about what makes them work, and if you like, make a list of "keys to success" for each element.

1. **The Lead**

   What makes a good lead? What is your all-time favorite lead?

2. **Conclusion**

   How should the writer leave the reader feeling? What is the best conclusion ever written—based on what you've read so far?

3. **Title**

   What makes a title grab our attention? What kinds of titles turn us off? Have you ever decided to read a book (or not) based solely on the title?

4. **One "just right" word**

   Try this. Choose any favorite book. Open it at random and read one paragraph aloud. Chances are you'll find at least one "just right" word in that paragraph. How does that happen?

Step 2: Making the Reading-Writing Connection

Book writers know the importance of strong leads and conclusions, and from them we can learn many lessons about getting a reader's attention through these important elements. Following are the lead and conclusion from Sid Fleischman's book *Escape!*—a memoir of magician Harry Houdini. Think for a moment how you might begin and end an essay on Houdini, and then consider Fleischman's choices.

Lead

Not long ago, the breast pocket snipped from a man's pajamas came up for auction in New York City. Immediately, bids around the room erupted like doves flushed from cover. (p. 1)

Conclusion

Not bad for a kid who used to roll up his cuffs and say, "There ain't nothing up my sleeves." (p. 202)

(From *Escape! The Story of the Great Houdini* by Sid Fleischman. 2006. New York: HarperCollins, pp. 1, 202.)

You may not have read Fleischman's book yet—but just from these two snippets, can you tell anything about Fleischman's attitude toward his subject? Do you think he finds Houdini interesting? Read the lead one more time. What questions does it raise in your mind? Look again at the conclusion, especially the words "Not bad." What do these words suggest about Houdini's achievements? Does anything in the voice of these short passages offer you a clue about Fleischman's feelings about Houdini?

Step 3: Involving Students as Evaluators

Ask students to review Samples A and B, looking and listening for strong leads, conclusions, and titles. Note the word choice as well. Which author does a better job of using these skeletal elements of writing to get and hold a reader's attention? Which one seems to be writing mostly just to get it done? Have students work with a partner, highlighting leads, conclusions, or words they find striking—and discussing ways to revise what is not working.

Discussing Results

Most students should find Sample A stronger. Discuss differences between the two pieces, asking students to consider ways of revising Sample B by changing the lead, conclusion, title—or all three. Ask them if they were only going to revise one word, which one it would be. A suggested revision of Sample B is provided, with *several words revised* (to illustrate possibilities).

Step 4: Modeling Revision

- Share Sample C (*Whole Class Revision*) with students. Read it aloud.

- Ask whether this writer does a good job of using the lead, conclusion, and title to make a strong impression on the reader. (Most students should say *no*.)

- Brainstorm ways of revising the lead, then the conclusion, then one word within the text, and finally, the title.

- Try to make all your revisions within five minutes—or come as close as you can. Check your final draft by reading it aloud.

Step 5: Revising with Partners

Share Sample D (*Revising with Partners*). Ask students to follow the basic steps you modeled with Sample C. *Working with partners,* they should:

- Read the passage aloud, focusing on the lead, conclusion, title—and secondarily, word choice.

- Highlight one or two words that could be stronger.

- Revise by drafting (in this order) a new lead, new conclusion, new title, and one or two "just right" words. (Ask students to try fitting all their revision work into five minutes, if possible. Allow more if they need it, but time them so they know how long they've spent.)

- Read their revisions aloud to hear the impact of their changes.

Step 6: Sharing and Discussing Results

When students have finished, ask several pairs of students to share their revised passages aloud. Which have the strongest leads? The strongest conclusions? The catchiest titles? Talk about the five-minute "limit" (with more time for those who need it). How much can a quick reviser actually accomplish in five minutes? If you wanted to be truly reflective about your writing, how much time would you need? (Answers to this will vary greatly.)

Next Steps

- Invite students to try five-minute revisions on their own work—with the understanding that they may do more at another time. Talk about how much a writer can accomplish in a limited time, given a plan and sufficient focus on the task.

- Watch and listen for strong leads, conclusions, word choice, and titles in the literature you share aloud. Pay particular attention to leads and conclusions that go together—sometimes the writing comes full circle, so that the conclusion echoes ideas introduced in the lead. Recommended:

  - *Escape! The Story of the Great Houdini* by Sid Fleischman. 2006. New York: HarperCollins.

  - *My Thirteenth Winter: A Memoir* by Samantha Abeel. 2003. New York: Scholastic.

  - *No More Dead Dogs* by Gordon Korman. 2000. New York: Hyperion Books.

  - *Stargirl* by Jerry Spinelli. 2000. New York: Alfred A. Knopf.

- *For an additional challenge:* The five-minute plan presented in this lesson is only one possibility for quick revision. Ask resourceful students to come up with a plan of their own: two to five important things a writer can do within five minutes or less. Ask them to "field test" it with your class. Does it work?

Sample A

Strong lead?
Strong conclusion?
Good title?

Thanks for Listening

I suppose almost everyone is influenced by his or her father—whether for good or bad. In my case, the influence has been a good one, and it's mostly for a small reason many people might overlook. My dad is the best listener I have ever known or seen.

Dad chose his profession, behavioral psychology, in order to help people. Lots of people have lofty goals like this, but I think it takes a listener to turn those goals into reality. Dad helps couples find ways to talk civilly to each other because they learn to hear not just words, but the hurt or frustration behind them. He helps teenagers build self-confidence by finding listeners in their own lives—a friend, sibling, or someone who will give you a minute of undivided attention. Occasionally, he guides someone into a new career because they learn to listen to their *own* internal voice—and they discover that their occupational choices are actually in conflict with their own goals, and produce stress. "A lot of headaches," Dad always says, "come from not listening to yourself."

My dad typically works 60 to 70 hours a week, but still makes time for his family. I see how tired he is, yet he'll plan a hike—or just a backyard barbecue. If I need to talk, he'll stop what he's doing, pull up a chair, and lean in, like he really cares what I have to say. He doesn't interrupt—as I see many other parents do. He thinks about what *I've* said before *he* speaks.

I have no idea, as yet, whether I will be a behavioral psychologist. Dad says I should take my time making this decision, and I will. I know one thing, though: I will be a good listener.

Sample B

My Most Memorable Experience

The most memorable experience I have had was when our family took a trip to Australia and we had a chance to go snorkeling on the Great Barrier Reef.

In case you do not know, the Great Barrier Reef is the largest living thing on the planet. It is made up mostly of coral, which is an animal (as I learned from our guide) and is alive, even though it does not move. Coral larvae attach themselves to something, such as a rock, sunken ship, or other coral, and the colony grows and grows. In the case of the Great Barrier Reef, the ocean temperatures and sunlight have provided the right conditions for the reef to grow to its amazing size— more than 1600 miles long. It did not look the way I expected. I thought every part of it would be under water, but actually, there are over 900 islands, so when you sail through it, it is like entering another world.

The water is extremely clear—which our guide explained is important so that the coral algae get the light they need to make food. They are the first link in the food chain. We could see octopuses, thousands of clown fish and yellow tang, small sharks, starfish, and some jellyfish. Some creatures are dangerous, and our guide told us what to watch out for. She also told us not to step on the coral. It looks hard and tough, but it is really fragile.

We had an amazing time, and I will never forget my trip to the Great Barrier Reef. Everyone should get to see this great work of nature.

Revision of Sample B

Trip to Another World
~~My Most Memorable Experience~~

~~The most memorable experience I have had was when our family took a trip to Australia and we had a chance to go snorkeling on the Great Barrier Reef.~~ Imagine floating through clouds of clown fish, or going nose to nose with a small shark. That's what it's like to snorkel the Great Barrier Reef, just off Australia's coast.

In case you do not know, the Great Barrier Reef is the largest living thing on the planet. It is made up mostly of coral, which is an animal (as I learned from our guide) and is alive, even though it does not move. Coral larvae attach themselves to something, such as a rock, sunken ship, or other coral, and the colony grows and grows. In the case of the Great Barrier Reef, the ocean temperatures and sunlight have provided ideal ~~the right~~ conditions for the reef to grow to its impressive ~~amazing~~ size—more than 1600 miles long. It did not look the way I expected. I thought every part of it would be under water, but actually, there are over 900 islands, so when you sail through it, it is like entering another world.

The water is extremely clear—which our guide explained is important so that the coral algae get the light they need to make food. They are the first link in the food chain. We could see octopuses, thousands of clown fish and yellow tang, small sharks, starfish, and some jellyfish. Some creatures are dangerous, and our guide told us what to watch out for. She also told us not to step on the coral. It looks indestructible, ~~hard and tough,~~ but it is really fragile.

~~We had an amazing time, and I will never forget my trip to the Great Barrier Reef. Everyone should get to see this great work of nature.~~ Since that trip I've often wondered if the Great Barrier Reef is a place my grandchildren will be able to visit on one of their "most memorable adventures."

Sample C: Whole Class Revision

Strong lead?
Strong conclusion?
Good title?

A Great Invention

What is the greatest invention of all time? Good question! Some people might think of penicillin, or even the lightbulb. Wrong! The greatest invention of all time, by far, is the computer. Just think about it.

Computers allow us almost instant access to information that we would once have had to spend hundreds of research hours to get. In addition, computers are the best record keepers in history. On one small disk you can keep enough data to fill a whole room with the old-fashioned record keeping systems. To say computers have changed communication is an understatement. We use them to do research, talk to each other, and hold virtual meetings with people located at all different parts of the globe. If you had told people two hundred years ago that they could buy European or Chinese goods with a keystroke, they would have thought you were insane. Yesterday's insanity is today's common occurrence.

Of all the many amazing and wonderful inventions people have come up with, nothing surpasses the computer.

Sample D: Revising with Partners

Strong lead?
Strong
conclusion?
Good title?

My Favorite Place

So many places are special to me that it is hard to focus on just one. I love New York City with its bustling sidewalks and Broadway charm. I love my grandmother's house, with its old creaky stairs and attic full of treasures. But for me, nothing is as special as "home," and my "home" has always been outdoors, in the wilderness.

I'm not very tolerant of noise. It gives me headaches and creates tension. I suspect others feel this way, too. I like the softer sounds of nature: Canada geese flying overhead, water running over rocks, frogs and crickets chirping in the moments before darkness falls. Nothing beats a vast expanse of star-covered sky for a view. No feather bed compares to the comfort of a good sleeping bag stretched over soft earth.

The wilderness is my home. It's also my favorite place to be.

Suggested Revisions of C and D

Sample C: Whole Class Revision

Try Living Without One
~~A Great Invention~~

What is the greatest invention of all time? ~~Good question! Some people might think of penicillin, or even the lightbulb. Wrong! The greatest~~

To answer that question, think of the things you'd least like to live without, and list them in order. Chances are, computers would be right at the top of that list.

~~invention of all time, by far, is the computer.~~ Just think about it.

Computers allow us almost instant access to information that we would once have had to spend hundreds of research hours to ~~get.~~ uncover. In addition, computers are the most accurate and thorough ~~best~~ record keepers in history. On one small disk you can keep enough data to fill a whole room with the old-fashioned record keeping systems. To say computers have ~~changed~~ revolutionized communication is an understatement. We use them to do research, talk to each other, and hold virtual meetings with people located at all different parts of the globe. If you had told people two hundred years ago that they could buy European or Chinese goods with a keystroke, they would have thought you were insane. Yesterday's insanity is today's common occurrence.

~~Of all the many amazing and wonderful inventions people have come up with, nothing surpasses the computer.~~ The toothbrush, the light bulb, the television, the camera—and the computer: Try going without all of them, and see which one you reach for first.

Sample D: Revising with Partners

Home Is Where the Sleeping Bag Is
~~My Favorite Place~~

~~So many places are special to me that it is hard to focus on just one~~

recall loving
I ~~love~~ New York City with its bustling sidewalks and Broadway charm.

recall hours spent exploring
I ~~love~~ my grandmother's house, with its old creaky stairs and attic full of

"home" is the place that calls you back,
treasures. But ~~for me, nothing is as special as "home," and my "home"~~

and I am always called back to
~~has always been outdoors, in~~ the wilderness.

I'm not very tolerant of noise. It gives me headaches and creates

agree.
tension. I suspect others ~~feel this way, too~~ I like the softer sounds of

bubbling
nature: Canada geese flying overhead, water ~~running~~ over rocks, frogs

and crickets chirping in the moments before darkness falls. Nothing

star-strewn
beats a ~~vast expanse of star-covered~~ sky for a view. No feather bed

body hugging luxury   pine-needle upholstered
compares to the ~~comfort~~ of a good sleeping bag stretched over ~~soft~~ earth.

~~The wilderness is my home. It's also my favorite place to be~~

In the revised edition of *Hatchet,* author Gary Paulsen says
he thinks and feels better when he can "slip into the trees and
disappear from the rest of the world." I think that sums it up.

Author's Note: The quotation is from Gary Paulsen,
Hatchet. 2007. New York: Simon and Schuster, p. 64.

Which Person Is on Deck?

Trait Connection: **Conventions**

Introduction (Share with students in your own words—or as a handout.)

A writer can speak from any of three different perspectives:

- **First person:** *I, we, me, us*
- **Second person:** *you*
- **Third person:** *he, she, they, it, one, people, a person, Frank, Betty,* etc.

First person (*I, we, me*) is the logical choice when the writer is speaking directly about him or herself, as in this note:

I love you, Bill. I always will. Love, Dorothy

Second person (*you*) is handy for talking directly to the reader, as when a writer is giving directions. It can be spoken or implied:

When you come to the old barn, take a left. (*you* spoken outright)

Turn left at the old barn. (*you* implied)

Third person (*he, she, they, it, Bill, people*) is used when the writer is talking about someone or something else. The person or persons *doing the action* are more important than the *speaker*—and thus take center stage:

It is dangerous to ski the back country unless a person knows how to judge avalanche danger.

People have a right to express their opinions.

Tom was walking down the dark corridor when suddenly, he saw a shadow.

Two conventional problems arise with the use of first, second, and third person. The first—which we'll deal with in this lesson—is shifting randomly from one to the other, as in these sentences:

I love swimming because you really get into it.

I had to give up the grapefruit diet because you can't stick with it.

Wait a minute. *Who* gets into swimming—the writer or the reader? *Who* can't stick to the grapefruit diet? This switcheroo problem can be fixed in one of two ways, depending on the meaning. If the writer is *really* talking about himself (or herself) personally, individually, then it's important to stay with *first person*:

I love swimming because I really get into it.

But sometimes a writer is really talking about "people in general," as in this example:

Frank never dives into shallow water because you can injure yourself that way.

This writer has shifted from third person (Frank) to second person (you). Who does she mean when she says *you?* She's not really talking about Frank himself anymore, nor about *you*, the reader. When she says *you*, what she really means is *people in general*. So her sentence can be revised as follows:

Frank never dives into shallow water because people can injure themselves that way. OR

Frank never dives into shallow water because a person can injure him- or herself that way.

The first sentence is less awkward because "people" takes a plural pronoun, "themselves." When you write "a person" or "one," you need to allow for the possibility that the person may be male or female. Notice that the second correction includes two pronouns: "himself or herself." It's perfectly correct. It's just a bit more cumbersome. (The second problem, by the way, involves using *I* or *you* when third person, for reasons of formality, is preferred. We'll deal with that problem in the next editing lesson. For now, let's focus on keeping point of view—first person, second person, or third person—consistent.)

Teaching the Lesson (General Guidelines for Teachers)

1. Share the examples above, or make up your own examples to acquaint students with first, second, and third person, and to discuss problems of shifting person (*I* to *you*, *Frank* to *you*).

2. Point out that a shift in person sometimes affects the form of the verb: *I go, you go, she goes, he goes, they go.*

3. Share the editing lesson on the following page. Students should read the text aloud, looking and listening for shifts in person.

4. All shifts should be corrected to reflect the writer's likely meaning. In other words, is the writer talking about him- or herself (I)? About the reader (you)? Or about an individual (Frank) or people in general (people)?

5. Ask students to edit individually first, then check with a partner.

6. When everyone is done, ask them to coach you as you edit the same copy.

7. When you finish, read your edited copy aloud, discussing your choices; then compare your edited copy with our suggested text on page 113.

Editing Goal: Edit for 7 shifts in person.
Follow-Up: Check for appropriate use of first, second,
and third person in your own work.

Editing Practice

Correct inappropriate shifts in person.

I always order an extra large salad, but you get a really small salad every time! I have tried to explain my problem, but you just *can't* make the server understand. I finally figured out the solution—you just have to point to the right-sized bowl!

My friend Ann has a problem, too. In that restaurant, you can't order things that aren't on the menu. Ann wanted cooked spinach, but you couldn't get it. I even spoke to the manager, but you still couldn't get it. I guess sometimes you just have to know when to give up!

Edited Copy

7 inappropriate shifts in person corrected.

I always order an extra large salad, but ~~you~~ I get a really

small salad every time! I have tried to explain my problem,

but ~~you~~ I just *can't* make the server understand. I finally

figured out the solution—~~you~~ I just have to point to the right-

sized bowl!

My friend Ann has a problem, too. In that restaurant,

~~you~~ a person can't order things that aren't on the menu. Ann wanted

cooked spinach, but ~~you~~ she couldn't get it. I even spoke to the

manager, but ~~you~~ she still couldn't get it. ~~I guess~~ Sometimes

~~you~~ a person just ~~have~~ has to know when to give up!

Revising for the "Watcher"

Trait Connection: **Voice**

Introduction

If you're like most people, you are not as comfortable with an audience of strangers as you are with a friend on the phone—and as a result, you may hold your voice in check, making your writing sound quiet, reserved, even encyclopedic. A good antidote for encyclopedic writing is to imagine yourself writing to someone you know and trust, someone who cannot *wait* to read what you have written—a parent or grandparent, relative, friend, sibling, or teacher. Picture that person clearly in your mind, and write what you think he or she would *love* to read. That person is your "watcher." As you write to him or her, listen to the voice emerge.

Teacher's Sidebar . . .

Voice is the single most powerful tool a writer has for keeping readers engaged. Thus knowing one's audience is vital. A broad audience can be hard to picture, however, whereas a single person is not. In *Radical Reflections*, teacher/writer Mem Fox tells us how important a "watcher" can be for any writer: "Whenever I write, whether I'm writing a picture book, an entry in my journal, a course handbook for students, or notes for the milkman, there's always someone on the other side, if you like, who sits invisibly watching me write, waiting to read what I've written. The watcher is always important" (1993, p. 9).

Focus and Intent

This lesson is intended to help students:

- Understand the importance of writing to a "watcher."
- Practice writing to a specified audience.
- Revise a flat piece of writing by revising it to speak to their own "watcher" or "best listener."

Teaching the Lesson

Step 1: Who's Watching?

Share the Mem Fox quotation from the Teacher's Sidebar, and briefly discuss the value of writing to a "best listener" or "watcher," as Mem Fox calls her personal audience. Talk about the fact that a writer's "watcher" might change from one piece of writing to another—what is important is getting a strong mental picture of this person prior to writing. Brainstorm a brief list of potential "watchers" from pop culture—people your students do not know personally, but feel they "know" well enough to envision as a personal audience. Think of writers, performers, politicians, television news anchors or other celebrities, and local people who are admired or might be in the news. *Choose people about whom students have a very positive feeling*. Ask each student to choose one watcher from this list, and then to revise the following flat piece of writing as if writing a note *to that watcher*. Read a few results aloud—and see if you can guess who the watcher might be! (*Note:* It is *not* necessary to retain every detail from the original, but revisers should maintain the general sense of the passage.)

> *The common wombat is found in both Australia and Tasmania. It is a marsupial. Its scientific name is Vombatus ursinus. The common wombat can weigh from 45 to 85 pounds, and has short legs, a heavily muscled body, and thick fur. They are vegetarians. They sleep a lot.*

Step 2: Making the Reading-Writing Connection

A conversational tone is fairly easy to achieve in narrative or other personal writing, in part because the author is often writing about what he or she knows best—personal experience and personal feelings. In *Diary of a Wimpy Kid*, author Jeff Kinney takes on the persona of middle school student Greg Heffley—whose mom has just bought him a diary. With the very first entry, on a Tuesday in September, he strikes up a rapport with the reader by sharing his feelings bluntly:

Sample

First of all, let me get something straight: This is a JOURNAL, not a diary. I know what it says on the cover, but when Mom went out to buy this thing I SPECIFICALLY told her to get one that didn't say "diary" on it.

(From *Diary of a Wimpy Kid* by Jeff Kinney. 2007. New York: Amulet Books, p. 1)

Notice, however, how author and biologist Sneed B. Collard goes for the same kind of rapport in an informational piece—even more of a challenge. He shares facts, all right, but puts his own conversational spin on them, as if he and the reader were walking along beside the wombat compound, having a chat. You might compare your wombat passage to Collard's:

Sample

Smart. Strong. Stubborn. Square. That pretty much sums up the wombat.
> *Three species of wombats live in different parts of Australia. They look like furry tractors with legs. Wombats are large animals, sometimes exceeding three feet in length and weighing more than eighty pounds. They tend to be shy, but are compact and heavily muscled. This serves them well when they are busy with one of their favorite activities—burrowing.*

(From *Pocket Babies and Other Amazing Marsupials* by Sneed B. Collard III. 2007. Plain City, OH: Darby Creek Publishing, p. 36.)

Who do you suppose the "watcher" might be for each of these writers? Sometimes a dedication gives us a clue. Collard's book is dedicated to his daughter Tess—who was a toddler at the time it was published. Might he picture her reading it at some point?

Step 3: Involving Students as Evaluators

Ask students to review Samples A and B, looking and listening for writing with a conversational voice. Which writer seems to be writing to a "watcher"? Which one seems to be writing to no one in particular? Have students work with a partner, highlighting moments of voice and making marginal notes about moments that could be strengthened.

Discussing Results

Most students should find Sample B stronger. Discuss differences between the two pieces, asking students to consider ways of revising Sample A by identifying a "watcher" (who can be anyone at all, so long as it's someone *specific*), and writing as if to that person. A suggested revision of Sample A is provided.

Step 4: Modeling Revision

- Share Sample C (*Whole Class Revision*) with students. Read it aloud.

- Ask whether this writer seems to be writing to a "watcher." (Most students should say *no*.)

- Brainstorm a particular watcher that will work for this piece. Then revise by either rewriting parts of the piece, or (as we have done in our example) starting over but retaining the same content.

- Remind students that it is fine to add new information about the Statue of Liberty.

- Check your final draft by reading it aloud—and comparing it to our sample revision if you wish.

Step 5: Revising with Partners

Share Sample D (*Revising with Partners*). Ask students to follow the basic steps you modeled with Sample C. *Working with partners,* they should:

- Read the passage aloud, listening to the voice, and asking whether it is conversational—or flat.

- Decide whether to revise by changing specific passages, or simply rewriting while retaining the original meaning (this is our approach).

- Choose a watcher to whom the piece will be written. It should be someone both people know well enough to get a clear mental picture of and a feeling for what this person would respond to as a reader.

- Revise by drafting identified sections of the piece—or by rewriting the whole piece in a more conversational voice. It is fine to add additional information about wolves.

- Read the revision aloud to test the voice: Does it speak to the identified watcher?

Step 6: Sharing and Discussing Results

When students have finished, ask several pairs of students to share their revised passages aloud. Which have the most conversational voice? Did any teams choose the same watcher? What can you tell about the watcher just by listening to the piece?

Next Steps

- Invite students to rewrite any personal piece after identifying a specific watcher—and to note how the voice changes when a writer has a specific audience in mind.

- Imagine who the watcher might be for any book or other literature that has strong voice. Be sure to check out both fiction and nonfiction. Recommended:

  - *Diary of a Wimpy Kid* by Jeff Kinney. 2007. New York: Amulet Books.

  - *Pocket Babies and Other Amazing Marsupials* by Sneed B. Collard III. 2007. Plain City, OH: Darby Creek Publishing.

  - *The Adventures of Marco Polo* by Russell Freedman. 2006. New York: Arthur A. Levine Books.

  - *Living With Wolves* by Jim and Jamie Dutcher. 2006. New York: Mountaineers Books.

- *For an additional challenge:* One of the best and most challenging ways to build skill in creating and controlling voice is by shifting the audience—the watcher. Ask students who are seeking a challenge to write a piece for one audience—and then rewrite it for another. When they read the two aloud for the rest of the class, can student listeners tell which piece was written for which audience?

Sample A

The Hummingbird

Various species of hummingbird live throughout North and South America. They are only about the size of a human thumb. But they are very strong. Some have been known to live for over 15 years. They have particularly strong hearts. The hummingbird's heart represents about 20 percent of its body weight, making it proportionally heavier than the heart of other animals. Their hearts average about 500 beats per minute while perching, but can go as fast as 1,200 beats per minute under stress. Hummingbirds spend most of their time perching, though they visit up to 1,000 flowers per day seeking food.

Strong wings can carry the birds on 20-hour migratory flights. Hummingbirds' wings can rotate almost 180 degrees, allowing the birds to hover or turn rapidly. The wings vibrate up to 80 times per second and make a humming noise—hence the bird's name. Hummingbirds' feathers have very bright colors.

Author's Note: Information for this piece is based, in part, on "Flight of Fancy" by Michael Klesius. *National Geographic.* January 2007. Pages 114–129.

Sample B

Strong voice?
Who's the
watcher?

In Defense of Zoos

Many people are opposed to zoos—and it's easy to understand why. They peer through bars to see animals they picture as bold hunters—animals like cheetahs, lions, and tigers—condemned to a life of eternal boredom, lying listless on a rock or patch of concrete. What is the point?

Just this: Without the intervention of zoologists and biologists who observe and treat zoo animals, many species would likely go extinct. Well, cry the zoo opponents, they will go extinct anyway. Perhaps. But even if that is true, we may be able to slow the race to the finish line.

For all their faults—and there are many—zoos do some remarkable things. They help scientists explore the conditions under which various species thrive, so that people who care have a better shot at recreating those conditions in the wild. Most important, they draw attention to animals that are slipping out of existence—animals many people would not even know about if they did not visit a zoo.

Today's zoos are not like jails—for the most part. They include expansive compounds where animals roam over grass, climb rocks, or play in trees. That doesn't make them perfect, but it does make them better than they were even two decades ago. And it points us in the right direction.

Revision of Sample A

Small Body, Big Heart
~~The Hummingbird~~

If you've ever seen a hummingbird up close, chances are it was moving, its wings vibrating so rapidly (up to 80 times per second), that you could hear the characteristic "small jet engine" sound that gives the bird its name. The truth is, hummingbirds spend most of their time perched quietly, but at less than the size of a human thumb, they are hard to spot—except when zooming to and fro. Their iridescent wings are as colorful as the 1,000 flowers they visit daily, and human fans spend large amounts of time and money photographing and feeding them.

One of the most remarkable characteristics of this tiny creature is its powerful heart. The hummingbird's heart represents about 20 percent of its body weight, making it proportionally bigger than that of any other animal. Just think: the heart of the average human would need to approach *30 pounds* to compete. And while human hearts average 60 to 70 beats per minute, the hummingbird's heart can hit 500 when it's just sitting around—and up to 1,200 if it's chasing a rival or fleeing danger.

The strength of the hummingbird's wing muscles, in proportion to its size, would make a weight lifter green with envy. They can carry the small birds on 20-hour migratory flights, and are flexible enough to rotate almost 180 degrees, allowing hummingbirds to hover, retreat, and turn literally on a dime. The hummingbird's heart may be no larger than a cranberry—but it is the heart of a warrior.

> **Author's Note:** Information for this piece is based, in part, on "Flight of Fancy" by Michael Klesius. *National Geographic.* January 2007. Pages 114–129.

Sample C: Whole Class Revision

The Statue of Liberty

The Statue of Liberty was presented to the United States by France in 1886 as a gesture of friendship. It stands at Liberty Island, New York in New York Harbor. It welcomes visitors, immigrants, and travelers.

The statue is covered in copper, and is over 300 feet high. It was built to withstand strong winds. It sways slightly so it will not break. The copper surface badly eroded over the years, but was significantly renovated in the 1980s. Many Americans contributed to that effort.

Liberty holds a stone tablet in her left hand and a flaming torch in her right hand. On the tablet is the date of the United States Declaration of Independence: July 4, 1776.

The Statue of Liberty is recognized by people throughout the world, and is considered a strong symbol of the United States. It was once open to visitors who could climb a spiral staircase to the top. Now, because of fire safety regulations, only the museum and 10-story base are open.

Sample D: Revising with Partners

Wolves of Yellowstone

Wolves have been feared for many years. At one point they were hunted almost to extinction. An effort was made by scientists to restore the wolves to their native habitat by relocating a small pack in Yellowstone National Park.

Ranchers opposed the relocation. They feared the wolves would kill their livestock. Many visitors to the Park wanted the wolves brought in, however, believing it would make the park more interesting and naturally authentic.

The wolves adapted to their new habitat. Most preyed on injured or older elk and deer. A few rogue wolves *did* kill livestock, however. Some states favor a return to hunting. That could put the wolf in danger of extinction once again.

People who love wolves and those who find them a nuisance continue to argue about this issue.

Suggested Revisions of C and D

Sample C: Whole Class Revision

Symbol of Freedom
~~The Statue of Liberty~~

The Statue of Liberty—arguably the most recognized symbol of the US around the world—stands at Liberty Island in New York Harbor, where she welcomes visitors, immigrants, and returning travelers, holding a golden torch of light in one hand and clutching a stone tablet in the other. When asked what is written on that tablet, many citizens do not know. It is the date of the US Declaration of Independence—July 4, 1776.

Liberty rises an impressive 300+ feet, and visitors used to climb the whole way up a narrow spiral staircase for a chance to stand at the top and look out over the harbor. Perhaps they were startled to feel the statue sway a bit in the wind—but that flexibility actually keeps the enormous structure from breaking. Visitors who never made the climb have likely missed their chance; thanks to more rigid fire regulations, only the base remains open these days. But they can still view the statue as immigrants have seen it for years—from a boat cruising the harbor.

The statue's copper surface badly eroded over the years, diminishing the golden reflection that thrilled first-time tourists. But thanks to the generous contributions of countless Americans, it was significantly renovated in the 1980s. Liberty, presented to the US by France in 1886 as a gesture of friendship, is recognized throughout the world as a symbol of freedom and safe harbor.

Sample D: Revising with Partners

Villains—or Noble Hunters?
~~Wolves of Yellowstone~~

Wolves have had a reputation as killers for centuries, and in years past, people hunted them nearly to extinction. Fearing their disappearance, scientists made an effort to restore the wolves to their native habitat by relocating a small pack in Yellowstone National Park, where they could roam without the threat of being shot.

Ranchers vehemently opposed the relocation, arguing that the wolves would kill their livestock. Park visitors saw it differently. They wanted the wolves brought in to make the park both interesting and ecologically authentic. As it turned out, both sides had a point.

The wolves thrived, and while most preyed on injured or older elk and deer, a few rogue wolves *did* go after livestock. Outraged ranchers demanded the right to kill the predators. If they get their way, hunting restrictions could be lifted—potentially putting the wolf in danger of extinction once again.

For now, the wolves continue to roam the hills of Yellowstone, hunting skillfully, and thrilling park visitors—and the argument continues to rage.

Think It—But Don't Write It

Trait Connection: **Conventions**

Introduction (Share with students in your own words—or as a handout.)

As we saw in the last editing lesson, a writer can speak from three different perspectives: first person (*I, we*), second person (*you*), or third person (*he, she, they, people, a person,* etc.). In serious informational writing—meaning a researched report as opposed to a personal essay—use of first person or second person is often frowned upon. "Don't use 'I,'" you may be told. At the same time, you want your writing to sound friendly, human—even conversational. It won't if you write in a stiff, unnatural way:

> One wonders at the origin of stars.

You can keep the words "I" or "you" out of the picture and still sound human, though, with a little careful wording:

> People cannot help but wonder at the origin of stars.
>
> Stargazers often wonder how it all began.
>
> Human beings are hypnotized by stars.
>
> A person looking at the stars may wonder how they were formed.

There is always a way to transform an "I" or "you" sentence—though sometimes it requires some gymnastics. You may need to flip the sentence around, word things differently, or begin in a different spot. Here are three examples. Think about how you would revise each one to *think* "I" or "you" without saying it:

- I find elephants fascinating.

- It would take you five days to sail through all the plastic floating on top of the ocean.

- You may be wondering exactly how photosynthesis works.

Here are those same sentences with the "I-you" factor removed:

- Elephants are fascinating.

- It would take a ship five days to sail through all the plastic floating on top of the ocean.

- Photosynthesis has intrigued people for generations.

Teaching the Lesson (General Guidelines for Teachers)

1. Share the examples above, or make up your own examples to acquaint students with various strategies for eliminating "I" or "you" in more formal writing.

2. Remind students that it is important NOT to sacrifice the human voice in such writing. It helps, as author William Zinsser advises, to "think I," even when you don't write it.

3. Share the editing lesson on the following page. Ask students to read the text aloud, with the assumption that it is a formal researched piece, looking and listening for examples of *I* or *you*. They should find eight such examples.

4. In this paragraph, the assumption is that third person (*he, she, they, people, persons*) is preferred. All first or second person references should be eliminated—and this may take some restructuring or revision of the sentence as a whole.

5. Ask students to edit individually first, then check with a partner.

6. When everyone is done, ask them to coach you as you edit the same copy.

7. When you finish, read your edited copy aloud, talking about ways that you re-crafted sentences to eliminate first or second person; then compare your edited copy with our suggested text on page 128.

**Editing Goal: Edit to eliminate first or second person references.
Follow-Up: Check with an instructor to see when first or third
person point of view is preferred—and in making this decision on
your own, consider audience and the formality of the piece.**

Editing Practice

Check for use of first or second person.
Change first or second person to third person *consistently*.

Scuba diving is one of the most satisfying sports a person can take up. Beginners can easily qualify by passing a simple diving test that requires you to dive down 15 feet, using special breathing apparatus. Once under the water, divers get hooked—usually! You see large schools of colorful fish, and if you're lucky, you may get close to a green sea turtle. Diving is becoming one of America's most popular sports. If you decide to take it up, though, it is important to work with a qualified instructor and to dive where it is safe. You can be injured diving in water that is unclear, or in an area that has not been screened for hazards, such as scrap metal or debris from ships. I can't begin to describe how rewarding it is! You will love it!

Edited Copy

First or second person changed to third person consistently

Scuba diving is one of the most satisfying sports a person

can take up. Beginners can easily qualify by passing a

simple diving test that requires ~~you~~ them to dive down 15 feet,

using special breathing apparatus. Once under the water,

divers get hooked—usually! ~~You~~ They see large schools of

colorful fish, and if ~~you're~~ they're lucky, ~~you~~ they may get close to a

green sea turtle. Diving is becoming one of America's most

popular sports. ~~If you~~ For those who decide to take it up, though, it is

important to work with a qualified instructor and to dive

where it is safe. ~~You~~ An unwary diver can be injured diving in water that is

unclear, or in an area that has not been screened for

hazards, such as scrap metal or debris from ships. ~~I can't~~ It's all but impossible

~~begin~~ to describe how rewarding it is! ~~You will~~ Most people who try it love it!

Revising to Go Over the Top

Trait Connection: **Voice**

Introduction

Do you like to exaggerate? If so, that's a dimension of voice you can exploit—in certain situations. It does not usually work well in a serious informational piece because accuracy and authenticity are essential to good informational (or persuasive) writing. But in an essay, travelogue, poem, or personal narrative, it's OK to go "over the top" once in a while to create a striking image, powerful impression, or strong mood. Exaggeration, after all, happens when the writer is really impressed by an event (*The rat came at us like a small gray tank . . .*) or is emotionally involved (*My heart felt as heavy as a boulder . . .*). Comedians use exaggeration all the time. It often gives a comic spin to a situation that is not otherwise funny. Exaggeration works best in a situation with some emotional intensity. There is probably not much to be gained by exaggerating the experience of making toast—but bungee jumping may be another story entirely.

Teacher's Sidebar . . .

When it comes to exaggeration, it takes a while to develop an ear for how much is *too much*. So for a time, give students some free rein. Keep reading examples from the pros: Gary D. Schmidt, Roald Dahl, Jack Gantos, and others. To keep things from getting out of hand within a single piece, you might ask them to "go for it" in draft 1, and then cut back to the top two or three "over the top" moments in a second draft.

Focus and Intent

This lesson is intended to help students:

- Understand the concept of "over the top."
- Recognize exaggeration done for rhetorical effect.
- Revise a piece by using over the top exaggeration for rhetorical effect.

Teaching the Lesson

Step 1: Going Over the Top

You must really "go for it" to make rhetorical exaggeration work. It is not effective, for example, to write, "That dog must have weighed 40 pounds!" unless the reader knows it was a Chihuahua. But, "That dog must have weighed 400 pounds!" will work for virtually any breed. Have some fun with the following descriptions, revising them to go over the top. Brainstorm some possibilities, and choose your favorite for each example. The first one is done for you.

Description

The cat became angry when Emma dumped water on it.

Over the Top

When Emma dumped water on her cat, he suddenly sprouted three-inch fangs.

Description

We were supposed to be quiet during the test. Kieran dropped a book on my desk, and the sound caught everyone's attention.

Over the Top

_____

Description

Brianna had said it was three flights up to the top of the tower. It felt as if we had been climbing for a long time.

Over the Top

_____

Step 2: Making the Reading-Writing Connection

In *The Wednesday Wars*, Holling Hoodhood tells of his discomfort sitting through a whole battery of tests. The heat in his school has not been working, and he has dressed for sub-zero weather. As luck would have it, though, the radiators begin to work full-force during the tests—making the students less than comfortable:

Sample

The room was now downright tropical. And I had on thermal underwear—thermal underwear that was supposed to keep me warm in minus-ten-degree temperatures. And I was starting to sweat everywhere—even my fingernails—and I think that I was probably turning the color of the rusted radiators.

(From *The Wednesday Wars* by Gary D. Schmidt. 2007. New York: Clarion Books, p. 119.)

Which descriptive moment most captures your attention in this passage? Can you feel what it would be like to sit in that classroom trying to concentrate on math problems and reading passages? What if the author had said, "The room was really hot now, and getting worse. It must have been almost 75 degrees!" What do you think as a reader and critic? Does it pay to go over the top sometimes?

Step 3: Involving Students as Evaluators

Ask students to review Samples A and B, looking and listening for "over the top" exaggeration. Which author does a better job of using such exaggeration to create a vivid scene, experience, or image? Which one sticks more with the literal facts? Have students work with a partner, highlighting moments of exaggeration—and discussing which ones work well.

Discussing Results

Most students should find Sample A stronger—in terms of going over the top. Discuss differences between the two pieces, asking students to consider whether Writer A goes too far, or whether they enjoy this "over the top" approach. Ask what suggestions they have for livening up Sample B with a little "over the top" fun.

Step 4: Modeling Revision

- Share Sample C (*Whole Class Revision*) with students. Read it aloud.
- Ask whether this writer goes "over the top" or sticks with the literal truth. (Most students should say *literal*.)
- Brainstorm moments where a little "over the top" description could enliven the piece.
- Revise by introducing two or three "over the top" moments—that's enough unless you feel truly inspired. Check your final draft by reading it aloud.
- Compare your draft with ours if you wish, realizing that ours probably includes more "over the top" examples for purposes of illustration.

Step 5: Revising with Partners

Share Sample D (*Revising with Partners*). Ask students to follow the basic steps you modeled with Sample C. *Working with partners,* they should:

- Read the passage aloud, looking and listening for moments of "over the top" exaggeration.

- Highlight one or two moments that would become more vivid with an "over the top" approach.

- Revise by inserting two (or more) "over the top" moments.

- Read their revisions aloud to hear the impact of their changes.

- Compare revisions with ours if you wish, keeping in mind that students' revisions are likely to be more restrained than ours.

Step 6: Sharing and Discussing Results

When students have finished, ask several pairs of students to share their revised passages aloud. Which "over the top" exaggerations do listeners especially enjoy? Which teams went all out? Which used a bit more restraint? Talk about which approach (restrained or all-out) works best. Also discuss the kinds of writing in which an "over the top" approach is most appropriate.

Next Steps

- Invite students to try "over the top" exaggeration in any personal form of writing: e.g., essay, travel piece, review, friendly letter, personal narrative, poem, fable.

- Watch and listen for "over the top" exaggeration in the literature you share aloud. Recommended:
  - *The Wednesday Wars* by Gary D. Schmidt. 2007. New York: Clarion.
  - *Jack's Black Book* by Jack Gantos. 1997. New York: Farrar, Straus, and Giroux.
  - *No More Dead Dogs* by Gordon Korman. 2000. New York: Hyperion Books.

- *For an additional challenge:* The flip side of exaggeration is understatement. It's quieter—but just as emotionally charged, often funny, and far harder to achieve. Let students who are ready have a go at description that involves understatement: *The sight of a beached whale made a few onlookers turn their heads. Betty was thrilled with her new job—though less thrilled after she was fired. Having a wild boar running loose in the locker room took our minds off the performance test. Losing the presidency was a set-back for Senator Hartworthy.* Big event—understated response. That's the key. Give it a go.

Sample A

Over the top?
or Literal?

The Best Hotel

It was late when we checked into the hotel. That had a good and bad side, as it turned out. On the down side, we were so tired we could no longer stand upright without propping ourselves against the front desk. We were also too tired to remember our names, so we just scribbled any old thing. My friend Harry pointed out that it didn't matter since most people don't have legible writing anyway.

On the other hand, there were good things about checking in at night. It was dark, which made the less appealing features harder to see. We didn't notice that the walls hadn't been repainted since Lincoln was president, or that the mattress was scarcely thicker than high quality cardboard. I doubt we'd have wanted to stay if we had realized we were sharing the room with several dozen cockroaches, an army of spiders, and a rat the size of a small terrier. The spiders were at least quiet—and we only heard the cockroaches when they were busy setting up a buffet lunch with the corn chips and chocolate bars we'd brought. The rat, however, made enough noise to wake people in the next building. Every time we turned on the light, however, all of our "companions" vanished except for the rat, whose expression clearly said, "Are you guys still here?"

Sample B

A Scary Experience

Brad had promised his friend Pete he would go bungee jumping on Pete's birthday. Pete's parents were paying for the whole experience. Pete had been several times, and kept telling Brad it was very safe.

All the same, Brad felt more and more uneasy as they approached the jump-off spot. It was in the center of a bridge overlooking a wide, deep river, and the plunge was no more than 75 feet. Jumpers walked out on a small platform that didn't look all that sturdy, but the guide assured the boys it was very strong.

Pete wanted to go first. He got into the harness, and walked to the end of the platform. Within seconds, he was flying through the air, yelling at the top of his lungs. Then, just like that, he was out of the harness, calling up to Brad from the river bank to hurry up.

Brad felt weak in the knees. He inched his way out to the end of the platform, wondering if he could think of a creative way out of this situation. Nothing came to him. He didn't hear a thing the guide said. He didn't even feel himself jump. Suddenly he was flying toward the earth—and then he was bouncing back! It was amazing!

Revision of Sample B

Human Eagle
~~A Scary Experience~~

Brad had promised his friend Pete he would go bungee jumping on

Pete's birthday. Pete's parents were paying for the whole experience.

Pete had been several times, and kept telling Brad it was ~~very safe~~ **as safe as sitting at home on your couch.**

All the same, Brad felt more and more uneasy as they approached

the jump-off spot. It was in the center of a bridge overlooking a wide,

deep river, and the plunge was no more than 75 feet **but looked to Brad more like 30,000.** Jumpers walked

out on a small platform that ~~didn't look all that sturdy~~ **looked about as sturdy as a thin pizza crust,** but the guide

assured the boys it was ~~very strong~~ **as strong as a steel I-beam.**

Pete wanted to go first. He got into the harness, and walked to the

end of the platform **as calmly as if he were picking up the mail.** Within seconds, he was flying through the air,

~~yelling at the top of his lungs.~~ **screaming louder than a jet engine.** Then, just like that, he was out of the

harness, calling up to Brad from the river bank to hurry up.

Brad felt ~~weak in the knees. He~~ **his legs turn to rubber. With the enthusiasm of a caterpillar about to be eaten, he** inched his way out to the end of

the platform, wondering if he could think of a creative way out of this

situation. ~~Nothing came to him.~~ **Maybe he could say he was a doctor who'd left a patient in surgery—or a spy with an emergency mission.** He didn't hear a thing the guide

said. He didn't even feel himself jump. Suddenly he was flying

toward the earth—and then he was bouncing back! ~~It was amazing!~~
**He was a human yo-yo. He was an eagle—and it was
a thousand times better than he could have imagined.**

Sample C: Whole Class Revision

Over the top?
or Literal?

The Speech

Ali had been dreading the speech she was supposed to give on Parent

Night. She had been asked by the principal to talk about the importance

of having a strong athletic department in the school. Ali was selected

because she was a basketball All-Star, and was also on the school's track

team. Her friends said she was an amazing athlete.

The night of the speech, Ali didn't feel amazing at all. In fact, she

felt small and unimportant. When she walked out onto the stage, it

looked as if there were at least a hundred people in the audience. They

were all looking right at her. When she finally spoke, she knew her voice

was soft, but when the principal asked her to speak up, his voice

sounded as if he were shouting.

Then, something happened. People were suddenly smiling and

clapping, and Ali's fear just melted. She felt good. She felt in control!

Ali was not only a good athlete, but she was a great speaker.

Sample D: Revising with Partners

Over the top?
or Literal?

Be Prepared

Celia's mom is a worrier. Lots of moms are, but Celia's mom worries more than most. When we go somewhere, we have to call when we get there, so Celia's mom knows we arrived in good shape. We also call when we leave, so she knows when to expect us.

Recently, I found out that Celia took a course in first aid. Celia's mom was concerned that Celia or one of her friends could be injured, and none of us would know what to do. So far Celia has not had to use any of her first aid skills, but it is probably a good idea to be prepared just in case.

Most of us are talking about what it will be like when we drive. Not Celia, though. She probably won't drive for a long, long time. Her mom is too nervous about it. I guess she'll find some other means of transportation!

Suggested Revisions of C and D

Sample C: Whole Class Revision

Metamorphosis
~~The Speech~~

thought to herself that she would rather eat raw snails than give

Ali ~~had been dreading~~ the speech she was supposed to give on Parent Night. She had been asked by the principal to talk about the importance of having a strong athletic department in the school. Ali was selected because she was a basketball All-Star, and was also on the school's track team. Her friends said she was ~~an amazing athlete~~ her school's answer to Tiger Woods. They said she was a "lightning bolt" on the track.

The night of the speech, Ali ~~didn't feel amazing at all. In fact, she~~

about as important and courageous as a field mouse.

felt ~~small and unimportant~~ When she walked out onto the stage, it

half the people on planet Earth were

looked as if ~~there were at least a hundred people~~ in the audience. They

staring so intently she almost felt herself melting under their gaze.

were ~~all looking right at her~~ When she finally spoke, she ~~knew her voice~~

could barely hear her own "field mouse" voice,

~~was soft~~ but when the principal asked her to speak up, his voice

like thunder echoing through a canyon.

sounded ~~as if he were shouting~~

lightning really did strike.

Then, ~~something happened~~ People were suddenly smiling and clapping, and Ali's fear just melted. ~~She felt good. She felt in control!~~

~~Ali was not only a good athlete, but she was a great speaker~~ The mouse had disappeared, and left a tiger in its place. Ali felt as if she could talk all night. She never wanted to leave that stage.

Sample D: Revising with Partners

And the Oscar Goes to . . .

~~Be Prepared~~

Celia's mom ^could actually take home the Oscar for "best performance by a worrier in a non-stressful situation." is a worrier. Lots of moms are, but Celia's mom ~~worries~~

~~more than most.~~ When we go somewhere, we have to call ~~when~~ ^the very second we get

there, ~~so Celia's mom knows we arrived in good shape.~~ and give a full report of our condition from temperature to blood pressure. We also call

at the precise second ^~~when~~ we leave, so she ~~knows when to expect us~~ can accurately time our arrival at the designated destination.

Recently, I found out that Celia took a course in first aid. Celia's

mom was concerned that Celia or one of her friends could ^pass out from laughing too much or sprain a wrist playing video games, ~~be injured,~~ and none of us would know what to do. So far Celia has not had to use any of her first aid skills, but ~~it is probably a good idea to be prepared~~

~~just in case~~ you never know when one of us will take a bad fall off the couch!

Most of us are talking about what it will be like when we drive.

until she's at least 50.

Not Celia, though. She probably won't drive ~~for a long, long time.~~ Her

Until then,

mom is too nervous about it. I guess she'll ~~find some other means of~~

~~transportation~~ wind up riding the bus wherever she goes!

Putting It All Together
(Editing Lessons 10, 12, and 14)

Trait Connection: **Conventions**

Introduction (Share with students in your own words—or as a handout.)

In this lesson, you will have a chance to put skills from three editing lessons together. You will:

- Avoid jarring shifts in tense: *We **caught** eight fish; we **eat** like kings! (Should be **ate** like kings.)*

- Avoid jarring shifts in person: *I watched the snow fall, and **you** couldn't believe how deep it was getting. (Should be **I** couldn't believe how deep it was getting.) SIMILARLY, **I** had hoped to attend the basketball game, but **you** need to get tickets in advance. (Should be **people** [or **fans**] need to get tickets in advance.)*

- Avoid casual "I" or "you" references in formal informational writing—but do not sacrifice the voice:
  You'll love travel once you try it . . . becomes
  Most people love travel once they try it.

Teaching the Lesson (General Guidelines for Teachers)

1. Begin by reviewing any information covered in Lessons 10, 12, and 14 about which students may have questions.

2. Review practice sample sentences from Lessons 10 and 12, if that is helpful.

3. Encourage students to refer to Lessons 10, 12, and 14 as they work on Lesson 16. Also provide handbooks, if you wish.

4. Share the editing lesson on the following page. Students should read the passage aloud, looking *and listening* for opportunities to correct inconsistencies in tense or person, or to eliminate casual use of "I" or "you." Ask them to think of this as a formal informational piece, and edit accordingly.

5. Ask them to work individually first, then check with a partner.

6. When everyone is done, ask them to coach you as you edit the same copy, making any changes you and they decide are important. When you finish, compare your edited copy to the one on page 142.

Editing Practice

Edit to eliminate inconsistent tense or person.
Revise sentences to eliminate informal "I" or "you."

Columbus Day celebrates the "discovery" of America by Christopher Columbus. You probably believed that Columbus was one of the first explorers, if not *the* first, to make a successful round-trip voyage across the Atlantic and set foot on what is now American soil. New evidence uncovered in recent years shows, however, that Columbus is far from the first explorer. Many others preceded him. In addition, as you can see from historical research, both North and South America were home to remarkably advanced civilizations established by native peoples. In fact, early explorers from Europe and beyond are thunderstruck by early temples, aqua-systems, roadways, artwork, and other wonders. You could hardly believe your eyes. Unfortunately, many of those early wonders have been lost, and I doubt we will ever fully appreciate all the advancements in medicine, government, and astronomy made by those early cultures. I know that both the Incas of South America and the Aztecs of Central America are powerful civilizations. But you can see both of them weakened by war and by diseases like smallpox that are brought to the Americas by the Europeans.

Edited Copy

12 corrections

Columbus Day celebrates the "discovery" of America by Christopher

Columbus. ~~You probably~~ [For years, many people have] believed that Columbus was one of the first

explorers, if not *the* first, to make a successful round-trip voyage across

the Atlantic and set foot on what is now American soil. New evidence

uncovered in recent years shows, however, that Columbus ~~is~~ was far from the

first explorer. Many others preceded him. In addition, ~~as you can see~~

~~from~~ historical research, shows that both North and South America were home to

remarkably advanced civilizations established by native peoples. In fact,

early explorers from Europe and beyond ~~are~~ were thunderstruck by early

temples, aqua-systems, roadways, artwork, and other wonders. ~~You~~ They

could hardly believe ~~your~~ their eyes. Unfortunately, many of those early

wonders have been lost, and ~~I doubt we will ever~~ [people living today may never] fully appreciate all the

advancements in medicine, government, and astronomy made by those

early cultures. ~~I know that~~ Both the Incas of South America and the

Aztecs of Central America ~~are~~ were powerful civilizations. ~~But you can see~~

Both, however, were ~~of them~~ weakened by war and by diseases like smallpox that ~~are~~ were

brought to the Americas by the Europeans.

Revising the Persuasive Voice

Trait Connection: **Voice**

Introduction

What's the right voice to use in a written argument? That's almost a trick question because the word "argument" can be misleading. It calls to mind an image of people heatedly exchanging accusations, growing more outraged as their argument progresses. A written "argument," however, is not a fight. It's a clear, thorough presentation of issues in which the writer works to *persuade* the reader to take a particular stand or action. A good persuasive voice is a debate voice: compelling and passionate, but never angry or sarcastic. Of course, when a writer feels passionate about a topic, it's easy to get excited—but it's important not to let the excitement get out of hand. In the end, anger can weaken an argument by making a writer sound desperate. Do your homework so that you can write with the authority that comes from knowledge and experience. *That* kind of voice will invite readers to listen.

Teacher's Sidebar . . .

In crafting a strong argument, nothing takes the place of researching a topic thoroughly and knowing the evidence for both sides. Only a writer who has already made a meaningful decision can lead others in doing the same. So this lesson does not take the place of research. Rather, it is meant to show the importance of presenting good information in its best light—with a compelling, but dignified voice.

Focus and Intent

This lesson is intended to help students:

- Recognize the "right" voice for a strong persuasive argument.
- Distinguish between a passionate voice and an angry voice.
- Revise an angry piece to give it the right voice for a strong persuasive argument.

Teaching the Lesson

Step 1: Toning Down the Rhetoric

Most of us, in the heat of the moment, say things we do not mean at some point in our lives. "If only I could take that back!" you might think to yourself at such a moment. One of the great things about writing is that you *can* take things back; that's the power of revision. Read the following excerpts from persuasive essays carefully, imagining that you are on the "other side"—in other words, you're one of the people this writer is trying to persuade. Are you persuaded—or put off? Revise each example to tone down the rhetoric, saying the same thing in a way that is likely to compel readers, not offend them. The first one is done for you.

Angry Rhetoric

Anyone who thinks we should have year-round school is just not thinking at all—period.

Toned Down Version

Though year-round school has some advantages, those who carefully weigh both sides will oppose it.

Angry Rhetoric

People who argue that global warming is not aggravated by the use of fossil fuels are simply ignoring the evidence.

Toned Down Version

_____

Angry Rhetoric

Only one kind of vacation truly gives people a chance to appreciate nature, and that is camping.

Toned Down Version

_____

Step 2: Making the Reading-Writing Connection

In *The Dangerous Book for Boys*, authors Conn Iggulden and Hal Iggulden argue that building a treehouse is difficult, but more than worthwhile. You may or may not agree. Does the opening to their discussion provoke you—or compel you to listen?

Sample

Let's be blunt. Building a decent treehouse is really hard. It takes something like sixty man-hours start to finish and can cost more than $200 in wood and materials . . . You could spend the same amount on a video-game console and a few games, but the treehouse won't go out of date—and is healthier, frankly.

(From *The Dangerous Book for Boys* by Conn Iggulden and Hal Iggulden. 2006. New York: HarperCollins, p. 21.)

Can you tell from this passage how much the authors like treehouses? How would you describe the voice: angry, or just compelling? Maybe you're not quite ready to jump up and start hammering together your own treehouse—yet. But do you have a hunch you might be ready by the end of this article? Notice that the writers have already anticipated *one* counter-argument. What is it? We encourage you to read the whole chapter, titled "Building a Treehouse." You'll find that while most of it is a how-to piece, this chapter, like most writing, is a blend of genres. The writers lead with two persuasive paragraphs because they know that unless they can convince you that you *need* a treehouse, you're not likely to read further.

Step 3: Involving Students as Evaluators

Ask students to review Samples A and B, looking and listening for angry rhetoric. Which author tones down the rhetoric so that it is compelling—but not angry? Which one goes a bit too far and risks provoking or alienating readers? Have students work with a partner, highlighting angry moments—and discussing other ways to *say the same thing*.

Discussing Results

Most students should find Sample B stronger—because it reflects a strong persuasive voice, but never resorts to anger or sarcasm. Discuss differences between the two pieces, asking students to consider which moments need toning down, and how they might revise while still keeping the same position. (*For this lesson, ask students to assume the viewpoint of the writer, even if they do not agree personally with the argument. The challenge in this lesson is to revise without switching sides.*) One possible revision of Sample A is provided.

Note: The examples in this lesson are just that—examples. They do not necessarily reflect the opinions of the author or publisher.

Step 4: Modeling Revision

- Share Sample C (*Whole Class Revision*) with students. Read it aloud.
- Ask whether this writer projects an angry tone, or an appropriately compelling voice. (Most students should say *angry.*)
- Underline those moments where the rhetoric is too angry or sarcastic to be effective, and brainstorm ways to tone down the rhetoric *without changing the writer's meaning*.
- Revise by changing the language—but *be careful*. Don't tone the text down so much that the writer's sense of passion and conviction is lost.
- Compare your draft with ours if you wish, keeping in mind that your wording need not match ours—so long as it's compelling.

Step 5: Revising with Partners

Share Sample D (*Revising with Partners*). Ask students to follow the basic steps you modeled with Sample C. *Working with partners,* they should:

- Read the passage aloud, looking and listening for moments of angry rhetoric.

- Highlight two (or more) moments that would be better if toned down.

- Revise by changing the wording so that it is still convincing and authoritative without sounding angry. (Remind students to maintain the essential meaning of the text. They may add details if they wish.)

- Read their revisions aloud to hear the impact of their changes.

- Compare their revisions with ours, keeping in mind that their revisions need not match ours in any way.

Step 6: Sharing and Discussing Results

When students have finished, ask several pairs of students to share their revised passages aloud. Which teams did the best job of toning down angry rhetoric without losing the original meaning of the text or the sense of conviction a persuasive writer needs? Did any teams add new details or information? Talk about how voice and evidence work in balance to create a good argument.

Next Steps

- To what extent are beliefs shaped through research? Is it possible for a writer to begin his or her research believing one thing, and wind up on the other side of the argument? Invite students to research any of the topics presented in Samples A, B, C, or D in this lesson, and to write a new argument, presenting *either side* in a compelling voice.

- Watch and listen for both passionate and angry rhetoric in any writing you share aloud. Explore letters to the editor in both local and national newspapers. Which letters achieve the right tone? Which sound angry? Talk about their impact on readers. Which are most convincing?

- Pretend you are the editor of the paper receiving any of the letters you use as examples. Write a response.

- *For an additional challenge:* Achieving the right persuasive voice is always easier when a writer believes deeply in what he or she is saying. Invite students to practice this voice by writing a letter to the editor on any topic about which they have strong beliefs and feelings. Encourage them to write a draft, then do some research, and weave in any new findings. Share both letters and responses with the class.

Sample A

Strong voice?
Angry or compelling?

Rid the World of Plastics!

American consumers use an obscene amount of plastic. We play with plastic toys and eat from plastic dishes. Everything comes packaged and re-packaged in ridiculous, oversized, impossible-to-open, *ugly* plastic containers. Why do we need all this packaging? Are we so terrified of product tampering that we have to seal up everything from toys to cosmetics as if we were wrapping up mummies?

We need to wake up! Plastic, for anyone who has not figured this out, does not dissolve. We cannot just pack up our garbage and think we are done with it. How dumb can we get? Sure, some of it is recycled— but that is only a small portion of what we throw away. Much of it goes into landfills, where it hangs around longer than dinosaurs.

If we have *any* sense at all, we will stop buying *anything* made of plastic if there is an alternative. We will recycle all plastics—not just throw them in the garbage as if we didn't care about the earth. Finally, we will support research that looks for new ways to use recycled plastic. Maybe then our overly materialistic society will stand a chance.

Sample B

Strong voice?
Angry or compelling?

Lower the Speed Limit

The average speed limit on U.S. highways is 55 mph, or 65 mph on major freeways. Many people, especially those who commute long distances, would like to raise this speed to 75 mph in all areas where it is reasonably safe to do so.

It's easy to understand why they feel this way. Who enjoys long hours in traffic? An increase in the speed limit, however, could have serious and dangerous ramifications. Large numbers of people already drive five to ten miles *over* the speed limit. How many of us will feel safe on highways where half the drivers are going 80 to 85 mph, and shining bright lights on those who "poke along" at 75? Higher speed limits will sanction risk and rude behavior.

Safety is the biggest issue here, but it's not the only issue. We burn more fuel than we should even when people drive 55 mph or less. If we begin allowing people to go 75 mph regularly, they will use about 10 percent *more* fuel—at this critical time when automobile manufacturers have made only minimal efforts to increase fuel economy, and when we are running out of non-renewable resources like oil. Face it: Americans love cars, love driving, and love going fast. Let's not pander to this obsession by turning our roadways into raceways. If anything, we should *lower* the speed limit to save fuel, save money, and save impatient drivers from winding up as victims of their own love for speed.

Revision of Sample A

Rid the World of Plastics!

American consumers use ~~an obscene amount of plastic~~ far more plastic than we realize. We play with plastic toys and eat from plastic dishes. ~~Everything~~ Almost everything from toys to cosmetics comes packaged and re-packaged in ridiculous, oversized, impossible-to-open, *ugly* plastic containers we struggle to open. Why do we need all this packaging? ~~Are we so terrified of~~ If product tampering ~~that we have to seal up everything from toys to cosmetics as if we were wrapping up mummies?~~ is our primary fear, there must be a more environmentally friendly way to address it.

~~We need to wake up! Plastic, for anyone who has not figured this~~ The big problem with plastic—from an environmental standpoint—is that it ~~out~~ does not dissolve. We cannot just pack up our garbage and think we Some new age plastics, made from corn, do dissolve, and some plastic are done with it. ~~How dumb can we get? Sure, some of it is recycled—~~ our discarded plastic represents but that ~~is~~ represents only a small portion of what we throw away. Much of it goes into landfills, where it ~~hangs around longer than dinosaurs~~ grows into plastic mountains that remain intact for as long as dinosaurs roamed the earth.

Fortunately, there are steps we can take to improve the situation. First, we must ~~If we have *any* sense at all, we will~~ stop buying *anything* made of plastic if there is an alternative. ~~We will~~ Second, we must recycle all plastics—not just throw them in the garbage ~~as if we didn't care about the earth~~ so that they turn into an environmental problem. Finally, we must ~~will~~ support research that looks for new ways to use recycled plastic. ~~Maybe then our overly materialistic society will stand a chance.~~ We can live without plastic, but we cannot live without a healthy environment.

Sample C: Whole Class Revision

Think Before You Cut

> Strong voice?
> Angry or compelling?

Last year, a decrease in our school budget forced the district to make cuts. Unbelievably enough, they chose to cut art classes from the curriculum. Good grief! It's hard to believe anyone could seriously support such a mindless decision.

If you were to take a trip around the world, what would you be looking for? Art, right? People don't visit other countries to explore factories or freeways or sewer systems. *Hello!* They visit art galleries, parks beautified by sculpture, or theaters for the performing arts. They look at the architecture of cathedrals or other famous buildings that reflect a city's history. *History*—that will be the *next* thing cut, no doubt! People who don't care about art probably don't care about history either.

Maybe people who cut art from the curriculum just picture a bunch of kids waving paint brushes around. That's as far as their limited imaginations take them. Well, here's a news flash. Art is the very foundation of human culture. When we cut art classes, we lose the best chance we have to study who we are as human beings. Bring art back into our schools!

Sample D: Revising with Partners

Stop Illegal Downloading!

Maybe one day you're sitting at the computer and you think to yourself, "I love this song! I'll think I'll just download it for my collection." Stop right there—unless you're planning to pay for it! Stealing a song from the Internet is no different from stealing a CD out of the store. Either action makes you a thief, plain and simple. You're robbing the artist of his or her royalties, and that's no different from walking into a bank with a gun. And please don't argue that everyone on the face of the earth does it. That's just lame.

You might also argue that it's only one teeny tiny little song. What difference could *that* make? Are you kidding? That's like saying it doesn't hurt to just steal a *few* dollars. Let's try to hang onto one last shred of honesty and integrity in our culture, OK? Most songs cost less than a dollar to download. We can afford to pay for them and we should. We are paying for someone's time and creativity—which is the part downloaders don't stop to think of! Stop illegal downloading and do things right—or learn to live without music in your life.

Suggested Revisions of C and D

Sample C: Whole Class Revision

Think Before You Cut

Last year, a decrease in our school budget forced the district to make

cuts. ~~Unbelievably enough,~~ **Unfortunately,** they chose to cut art classes from the

curriculum. ~~Good grief! It's hard to believe anyone could seriously support such a mindless decision.~~ **We can only hope the district may be willing to rethink this decision.**

Picture yourself taking ~~If you were to take~~ a trip around the world. What would you be

looking for? ~~Art, right? People don't visit other countries to explore~~ **If you're like most travelers, you wouldn't be exploring**

factories or freeways or sewer systems. ~~Hello! They visit~~ **Instead, you'd be visiting** art galleries,

parks beautified by sculpture, or theaters for the performing arts. ~~They~~

You'd be studying ~~look at~~ the architecture of cathedrals or other famous buildings that

reflect a city's history. ~~History — that will be the next thing cut, no doubt! People who don't care about art probably don't care about history either.~~ **If we stop to think about it, history is preserved partly through art.**

~~Maybe people who cut art from the curriculum just picture a bunch of kids waving paint brushes around. That's as far as their limited~~ **When people try to picture art classes, they may see students sketching portraits or painting landscapes. Art is so much more than this, however.** ~~imaginations take them. Well, here's a news flash.~~ Art is the very

foundation of human culture. When we cut art classes, we lose the best

chance we have to study who we are as human beings. Bring art back

into our schools!

Sample D: Revising with Partners

Stop Illegal Downloading!

Maybe one day you're sitting at the computer and you think to yourself,

"I love this song! I'll think I'll just download it for my collection." Stop

~~and ask yourself whether you're willing~~ *Downloading*

right there ~~unless you're planning~~ to pay for it! ~~Stealing~~ a song from

illegally   *taking*   *without paying.*

the Internet is no different from ~~stealing~~ a CD out of the store. Either

deprives

action ~~makes you a thief, plain and simple. You're robbing~~ the artist of

his or her royalties, and that's ~~no different from walking into a bank with~~

~~a gun. And please don't argue that everyone on the face of the earth does~~

~~it. That's just lame.~~ *unfair.* We need to reward musicians and song

writers for their time and creativity.

Some people argue that downloading just one song illegally

makes no difference. ~~You might also argue that it's only one teeny tiny little~~

~~song. What difference could *that* make? Are you kidding?~~ That's like saying

We need to hold onto our

it doesn't hurt to just steal a *few* dollars. ~~Let's try to hang onto one last shred of~~

honesty and integrity ~~in our culture, OK?~~ Most songs cost less than a dollar

this small fee.

to download. We can afford ~~to pay for them and we should. We are paying for~~

~~someone's time and creativity — which is the part downloaders don't stop to~~

We must   *support the artists whose work we value—*

~~think of.~~ Stop illegal downloading and ~~do things right~~ or learn to live without

our lives.

music in ~~your life.~~

Putting Modifiers in Their Place

Trait Connection: **Conventions**

Introduction (Share with students in your own words—or as a handout.)

A modifier is a phrase, clause, or word that describes a noun, pronoun, or verb:

The clerk sold us a table <u>with spindly legs</u>. (*What kind of table?*)

<u>With grace and style</u>, Emily read us a very long poem.
(*How did Emily read?*)

<u>Intently</u>, we watched the tiger stalk its prey. (*How did we watch?*)

In all the preceding sentences, it is clear what the underlined modifier describes. There's no confusion. But notice something. In every single one of those examples, the modifier is *right next* to the word it modifies. That's a good habit to get into—like putting your keys in a safe place so you remember them every time. When writers let the modifier get too far from the word it modifies, a sentence can get confusing:

1. The teacher watched the class <u>laughing heartily</u>.
2. They thanked him for a great speech <u>at the end of the meeting</u>.
3. Shelly <u>only</u> wanted to eat popcorn.
4. We <u>almost</u> earned $10 washing cars.

In sentence 1, we cannot be sure whether the teacher or the class was laughing heartily. In sentence 2, was the person thanked after the meeting—or did the speech occur after the meeting? In sentence 3, the writer has told us that eating popcorn was all poor little Shelly asked out of life; but what the writer probably means was that picky old Shelly didn't want to eat anything *else*. Sentence 4 says that we had a chance to earn money washing cars, but we missed it; the writer probably means that we earned *just under* $10. Let's rearrange things to make all this clear:

1. *Laughing heartily,* the teacher watched the class ~~laughing heartily~~

At the end of the meeting,
2. ^ they thanked him for a great speech. ~~at the end of the meeting~~.

only
3. Shelly ~~only~~ wanted to eat ^ popcorn.

almost
4. We ~~almost~~ earned ^ $10 washing cars.

Here comes your chance to put some modifiers in their place. Misplaced modifiers are tricky, so read carefully. Ask yourself whether each sentence is clear. Do you know *exactly* what the writer is saying? Or, do you need to re-word the sentence to eliminate confusion?

Teaching the Lesson (General Guidelines for Teachers)

1. Share the examples above, or make up your own examples to acquaint students with strategies for correcting misplaced modifiers.

2. Remind students that it is important to read the passage aloud, and to double check the meaning of each sentence, one by one: *Even if you can tell what the writer meant, is that what he or she actually said?*

3. Share the editing lesson on the following page. Ask students to read the text aloud, looking and listening for misplaced modifiers.

4. Ask students to edit individually first, changing the word order of the sentence to make the reference clear in each case. Then they should check with a partner.

5. When everyone is done, ask them to coach you as you edit the same copy.

6. When you finish, read your edited copy aloud, talking about what each modifier refers to (you may wish to underline them); then compare your edited copy with our suggested text on page 157.

Editing Goal: Edit to eliminate 5 misplaced modifiers.
Follow-Up: Watch for misplaced modifiers in your own work.

Editing Practice

Check for misplaced modifiers.

Aunt Peach told us that she had worked as a librarian

during lunch. What a surprise! She said that she would take

us to meet the new librarian as she waved the waiter over.

We couldn't wait. Aunt Peach always told the best jokes.

She had us laughing by the time the waiter brought salads

on glass plates so hard our sides hurt. We asked Peach what

kinds of books she loved best. She confided that she loved

mysteries over dessert. She said she would also keep our

favorites in mind, if we had any. Thanks, Aunt Peach!

Edited Copy

5 misplaced modifiers corrected

During lunch,

Aunt Peach told us that she had worked as a librarian.

As she waved the waiter over,

~~during lunch,~~ What a surprise! She said that she would take

us to meet the new librarian. ~~as she waved the waiter over,~~

We couldn't wait. Aunt Peach always told the best jokes.

~~She had us laughing~~ By the time the waiter brought salads

she had us laughing

on glass plates, so hard our sides hurt. We asked Peach

over dessert

what kinds of books she loved best. She confided that she

loved mysteries. ~~over dessert,~~ She said she would also keep

in mind.

our favorites, ~~in mind,~~ if we had any. Thanks, Aunt Peach!

Revising to Define a Word

Trait Connection: **Word Choice**

Introduction

What do you do when you're reading and come to a word you don't know? Do you skim over it? Try to figure it out? Pause to look it up? If you're very lucky, and you happen to be reading something written by an author who thinks about his or her readers, you might find that you can figure out the meaning just by reading the passage carefully, sometimes more than once. The meaning of the word comes clear from the way the writer uses it. This is sometimes called making meaning clear "from context." It's a pretty neat writer's trick—one you'll want to think about using yourself. After all, many readers won't trouble to go to the dictionary or thesaurus. And if they don't take time to look a word up, and don't know what it means, they could misinterpret your message. Making meaning clear from context is just another way of being careful with the words you use.

Teacher's Sidebar . . .

It would become incredibly tedious to make the meaning of every word clear from context—and it is unnecessary. The reader, after all, shares *some* responsibility for determining meaning. But the responsibility for clarity falls mainly to the writer when he or she uses an unusual word, uses a word in an unexpected way, or uses a technical or scientific term that might not be familiar to many readers. This is always a judgment call—but too often, students write only for teachers, assuming knowledge of both topic and vocabulary. This is not a good habit. Remind students that good writers envision a broader audience, and write—always—to bring all readers into the conversation.

Focus and Intent

This lesson is intended to help students:

- Understand the concept of making meaning clear from context.
- Distinguish between passages in which the writer has made meaning clear—and those in which he/she has not.
- Revise a passage to make the meaning of a word clear from the way it is used.

Teaching the Lesson

Step 1: Searching for Meaning

In some of the following passages, the meaning of the **boldfaced** word is clear from the way in which it is used. You should be able to define the word, explain it, or come up with a synonym, even if it's a word you have not heard or used before. In other passages, the meaning of the boldfaced word is not clear. You might know it already; but the point is, if you didn't, you could *not* figure out the meaning from the passage. If that is the case, modify the passage to make the meaning of the word clear. Feel free to change any wording, or to add a sentence or example.

1. When the fire alarm sounded, people exploded from the building, running pell-mell, every which way. In the midst of this **tumult**, a three-year-old toddler was separated from her parents.

    ___ **Clear**   *tumult* means _____

    ___ **Unclear**   **Revision:** _____

    _____

2. Some people in the restaurant were engaged in a lively **repartee**.

    ___ **Clear**   *repartee* means _____

    ___ **Unclear**   **Revision:** _____

    _____

3. The tribe lived a **nomadic** life, constantly moving from place to place, in search of food, water, and pasture land for their animals.

    ___ **Clear**   *nomadic* means _____

    ___ **Unclear**   **Revision:** _____

    _____

4. He was such a **manipulative** person that it was difficult for him to make friends.

    ___ **Clear**   *manipulative* means _____

    ___ **Unclear**   **Revision:** _____

    _____

Step 2: Making the Reading-Writing Connection

Mattie, the hero of Jennifer Donnelly's book *A Northern Light*, collects words. She enters them in her journal, uses them in speaking—and hopes to use them as a writer one day. Most of the time, she gets her words from the dictionary, opening it at random to find her "word of the day" . . .

Sample

Wan, my word of the day, means having a sickly hue or an unnatural pallor. Showing ill health, fatigue, or unhappiness; lacking in forcefulness or competence. It has parents: the Old English wann, *for "dark" or "gloomy," and the German* wahn, *for "madness."* Wan *shows its breeding; it has elements of* wann *and* wahn *in it, just like the new kittens have elements of Pansy, the barn cat, and Shadow, the wild tom.*

(From *A Northern Light* by Jennifer Donnelly. 2004. New York: Harcourt, p. 85.)

Does Mattie show her love for words in this passage? Does she help readers understand the meaning of the word *wan*? Put her teaching to the test: See if you can either define the word, or use it in a sentence. If you can do this almost without thinking about it, the writer has done her job. By the way, in defining *wan*, does the author make the meaning of any other words clear also?

Step 3: Involving Students as Evaluators

Ask students to review Samples A and B, looking and listening for ways in which the writer makes the meaning of a word clear from context. Which author does a better job of this? Which one leaves readers dangling if they do not already know the meaning of a word? Have students work with a partner, highlighting words or phrases that provide a clear context for understanding a word's meaning. Encourage students to use a dictionary or thesaurus to explore the meaning of any words—whether they feel they know them already or not.

Discussing Results

Most students should find Sample A stronger. The writer makes a clear effort to make word meanings clear. Writer B, by contrast, uses words in a way that could leave readers guessing—unless they knew the word meanings well. Discuss differences between the two pieces, asking students to think about word meanings, and ways in which writer B could make meaning more clear. One possible revision of Sample B is provided. (*Note: In some cases, students may already know all word meanings well; for purposes of this lesson, however, they should try to imagine how they might respond if they did not know the meanings.*)

Step 4: Modeling Revision

- Share Sample C (*Whole Class Revision*) with students. Read it aloud.
- Ask whether this writer makes meaning clear from context—or leaves readers *potentially* confused (assuming they did not know word meanings already). (Most students should say *confused.*)
- Identify any word or words that the writer needs to make clear in order to be *certain* the message is understood.
- Look the words up in a dictionary and/or thesaurus and discuss the meanings. Play with the language a little, using the words in conversation or writing (practice sentences).

- Revise by changing the wording of a passage or adding a sentence or two to make the meaning of a word clear.

- Compare your draft with ours if you wish, keeping in mind that your revision need not match ours—so long as word meaning is clear.

Step 5: Revising with Partners

Share Sample D (*Revising with Partners*). Ask students to follow the basic steps you modeled with Sample C. *Working with partners,* they should:

- Read the passage aloud, looking and listening for words that need clarification in order to be certain the message is not misunderstood.

- Highlight at least one word that calls for such clarification.

- Look the word up in the dictionary and/or thesaurus, exploring the meaning and thinking of ways to make that meaning clear to a reader.

- Revise by changing wording and/or adding a sentence or two that would help a reader who did not know the word to understand it so well that he or she could then use it in speaking and writing.

- Read their revisions aloud to hear the impact of their changes.

- Compare their revisions with ours, keeping in mind that their revisions need not match ours in any way.

Step 6: Sharing and Discussing Results

When students have finished, ask several pairs of students to share their revised passages aloud. Which teams did the best job of making word meaning clear to readers? Which in-context definitions will actually help your students feel comfortable using the words in question?

Next Steps

- Try Mattie's strategy: Ask students to open a dictionary (or thesaurus) at random and choose a "word of the day" from the page. Then challenge them to find a way of defining that word so clearly (through writing, drawing, drama, or other performance) that students in the class will make the word their own—and not forget it.

- Practice the "clear from context" strategy using current vocabulary from math, science, or social science courses, and defining terms in a way that would be helpful for new students.

- When students share their writing in a response group, invite group members to listen for any words that are not clear from context. Ask them to write those words on 3×5 cards that can then be given to the writers after sharing. This feedback helps writers to know whether their message is getting through.

■ Watch and listen for unfamiliar words in the literature you share aloud. Add them to writing journals, if you wish. Talk about which authors do the best job of defining words by the way they use them—and which writers leave readers to figure things out for themselves. Recommended (for strong in-context definitions):

- *A Northern Light* by Jennifer Donnelly. 2004. New York: Harcourt.
- *Guts* by Gary Paulsen. 2001. New York: Random House.
- *The Wall* by Peter Sis. 2007. New York: Farrar, Straus and Giroux.

■ *The Wall* by Peter Sis is a graphic memoir for older students. It is based on the author's experience of growing up behind the Iron Curtain. Use this book to initiate an exploration and conversation about how graphics aid in the definition of words or concepts. Invite students to expand any definition through *drawing*.

■ *For an additional challenge:* Word definitions are particularly important in informational writing, where technical terms must be used with precision. Informational writers sometimes make definitions clear from context—but also use other strategies: a glossary of terms, for example, footnotes, or annotations. Ask students looking for a challenge to find a sample informational text that uses one of these strategies, and to use it as a model in creating an informational piece of their own that includes definitions (via glossary, footnote, or annotation) for at least five terms.

Sample A

Library Scheduled for Demolition
(A newspaper story)

The old Harny County Library on 3rd Street and Dickensen is scheduled for demolition next Thursday, May 5. Many patrons are expected to gather for a final goodbye as the building is torn down. The library has been in operation since 1898, and inspections have revealed growing structural frailties that render the building unsafe. After a walk-through on April 20, inspectors claimed the building was in a dilapidated condition, with floor braces not up to code, and decaying ceiling rafters that could—according to one authority—"give way at any moment."

The decrepit structure has been closed immediately in order to protect patrons. A crew experienced in dealing with decaying structures has been hired to relocate the library's collection of more than 20,000 books and other volumes. Materials will be housed, temporarily, in a local storage facility. Meantime, county officials are seeking a more permanent solution to the predicament posed by this sudden decision to destroy the county's old landmark. With luck, a new site will be identified soon.

Sample B

**Conundrum for Lifeguards
Press Release**

Visitors to South Beach are cautioned to be particularly

meticulous in reading warning flags. Last week's incursion

of noxious jellyfish has produced a conundrum for

lifeguards. Many divers and snorkelers are enjoying

viewing the unusual creatures and taking underwater

photographs. The stings from jellyfish can be toxic—even

lethal. Intrepid swimmers race happily past the flags,

plunging into the water, hoping for a good photo op. Said

one of the lifeguards, "They're simply oblivious."

Meaning clear
from context?
Readers left
confused?

Revision of Sample B

Conundrum for Lifeguards

Visitors to South Beach are cautioned to be particularly

(To put it bluntly, pay attention!)

meticulous in reading warning flags. Last week's incursion

of noxious jellyfish has produced a conundrum for

(who have never seen so many jellyfish invade these waters, and want beach visitors to have fun, but not at risk of their lives.)

lifeguards. Many divers and snorkelers are enjoying

viewing the unusual creatures and taking underwater

(not realizing the danger they face from even one poisonous sting.)

photographs. The stings from jellyfish can be toxic—even

seeming to fear nothing,   warning

lethal. Intrepid swimmers, race happily past the flags,

and plunge

~~plunging~~ into the water, hoping for a good photo op. Said

(to the danger. It's a real problem for us.")

one of the lifeguards, "They're simply oblivious.

Sample C: Whole Class Revision

Marble: The Real Deal

Marble is a metamorphic rock. It is found throughout the world, with particularly large deposits in Poland, Spain, Italy, China, and Greece. It is also found in some parts of the United States, including Texas and Colorado.

Throughout history, marble has been used in both architecture and sculpture. It is valued for its beauty, and also its durability. In some cultures—including the American culture—marble is often considered a symbol of elegance, prestige, and wealth.

Consumers should know that not every product labeled "marble" is the real thing. The term is often loosely applied to any durable stone or rock-like product that has a shiny surface. Real marble takes many years to form and is relatively rare. Hence its high price.

Sample D: Revising with Partners

Alluvium: The River's Gift to Farming

Alluvial deposits make agriculture possible—and profitable—in areas that border rivers directly. In Egypt, for example, agriculture has thrived for generations because of abundant alluvium.

Alluvium tends to increase in areas where water flows slowly or where the river makes turns. Alluvial deposits of gold or other precious metals are sometimes termed "placer" deposits.

Because alluvium varies in texture and color, it may influence the color of the river water itself. One example of this is the Mississippi River, sometimes nicknamed "Big Muddy."

Suggested Revisions of C and D

Sample C: Whole Class Revision

Marble: The Real Deal

Marble is a metamorphic rock. [one that has changed form over time.] It is found throughout the world, with particularly large deposits in Poland, Spain, Italy, China, and Greece. It is also found in some parts of the United States, including Texas and Colorado. **Marble is formed when rock such as limestone comes under great heat and pressure. Most of the fossils are destroyed, and any remaining sediment shows up as colored ribbons—sometimes termed "marbling."**

Throughout history, marble has been used in both architecture and sculpture. It is valued for its beauty, and also its durability. In some cultures—including the American culture—marble is often considered a symbol of elegance, prestige, and wealth.

Consumers should know that not every product labeled "marble" is the real thing. The term is often loosely applied to any durable stone or rock-like product that has a shiny surface. Real marble takes ~~many~~ literally eons [can only occur when the conditions are just right to make one kind of rock change into another.] ~~years~~ to form and ~~is relatively rare.~~ Hence its high price.

Sample D: Revising with Partners

Alluvium: The River's Gift to Farming

are the soil and silt gathered in one spot and dropped in another by a river or other moving water. Because they are so rich in minerals, these deposits

Alluvial deposits make agriculture possible—and profitable—in areas

that border rivers directly. In Egypt, for example, agriculture has thrived

for generations because of abundant alluvium—mineral-rich silt, clay, sand, and gravel left along the riverbanks of the slow moving Nile.

Alluvium tends to increase in areas where water flows slowly or making such spots potentially rich farm lands. where the river makes turns. Alluvial deposits of gold or other

precious metals, are sometimes termed "placer" deposits, are also common in areas where the water slows enough to let the heavier metals settle.

Because alluvium varies in texture and color, it may influence the

color of the river water itself. One example of this is the Mississippi

River, sometimes nicknamed "Big Muddy" because of the large amounts of silt and clay carried in its water. Alluvium makes the Mississippi Delta a very fertile region.

To Capitalize or Not

Trait Connection: **Conventions**

Introduction (Share with students in your own words—or as a handout.)

Capital letters were developed originally because they are eye catching. They provide signals to a reader. A capital tells a reader, for example, that a new sentence is beginning or that a word is a name. A *full sentence* following a colon also begins with a capital, while a single word or phrase does not. In addition, the pronoun "I" is always capitalized—perhaps because originally, printers feared that lower case "i" might get lost in the shuffle. Here are some examples of correct capitalization:

- Tom and I left for Arizona on Tuesday.

- Olivia told me she lived for one thing: She wanted to see a wild elephant up close.

- Ed lived for a different thing: doughnuts.

- While in New York, Sheila and I took time to see the play *Wicked*.

Sometimes writers get confused about whether or not to use a capital letter. For example, the word "president" is always capitalized when it refers to the President of the United States, but not when it refers to the president of a company—*unless* it is used as part of a name:

1. The President is addressing Congress at 2 p.m. today.

2. The president of the union wants to meet with corporate leaders.

3. The Board of Directors called for President Brown's resignation.

When deciding whether to capitalize, it is helpful to ask whether a reference is used as a name: *It is hot in the <u>desert</u>*. Versus: *Temperatures in the <u>Sahara Desert</u> may soar over 120 degrees*. In the first example, the writer is referring to deserts in general. In the second, the writer names a specific desert. Following are more examples that show this kind of distinction. Check your handbook for additional examples like these:

- We headed west. *(the direction)*
- Sean lives in the West. *(the name of the region)*

- Do you have a good doctor? *(referring to doctors in general)*
- Have you met Dr. Winslow? *(the name of a person)*
- I enjoy Brussels sprouts—especially with French fries. *(foods with regional names)*
- Let's go to the fair. *(not used as a name)*
- The Iowa State Fair begins next week. *(used as a name)*

You can correct capitalization errors (when the capital is missing) by either drawing a triple underscore beneath the letter that should be capitalized, or drawing a caret right into the letter and printing the capital above it, like this:

jon makes a living training ^laborador retrievers.

When a word is capitalized, but should not be, draw a slash mark through the capital, like this:

Eleanor got an A on her Social Studies Test.

Teaching the Lesson (General Guidelines for Teachers)

1. Share the examples above, or make up your own examples to acquaint students with *some* of the rules involving capitals.

2. Make sure everyone understands how to edit capitalization errors, whether it's a missing capital or a capital that should not be there.

3. Make sure students have access to a good handbook (*Write Source: The New Generation* published by Great Source Education is recommended) to which they can refer during the lesson.

4. Remind students to read the passage aloud, asking as they go, "Is this reference being used as a proper name?" Also remind them to look for missing capitals as well as capitals that are *not needed*.

5. Share the editing lesson on the following page. Ask students to read the text aloud, looking and listening for capitalization errors.

6. Ask students to edit individually first, then check with a partner.

7. When everyone is done, ask them to coach you as you edit the same copy.

8. When you finish, read your edited copy aloud, talking about the reasons behind each change; then compare your edited copy with our suggested text on page 173.

Editing Goal: Catch and correct capitalization errors.
Follow-Up: Watch for capitalization errors in your own work.

Editing Practice

Correct all capitalization errors.

we had an opportunity to interview Author Simon Rush,

who was on Location in yellowstone Park doing Research

for his upcoming Book titled *The History of The gray Wolf*.

Rush explained that he had traveled throughout the west,

particularly in the rocky mountain states, with one

objective: to observe Wolves in their Native Habitat. Much

of his original information came from the international wolf

center (IWC), located in Ely, minnesota. Thanks to a

Relocation Project, many wolves have been moved to the

park, where they have thrived, feeding primarily on rabbits,

Deer, and Elk. scientists from all over the Earth have visited

yellowstone in recent years, not only to observe the Wolves,

but to assess their Impact on the Ecology of the Area. A

group of scientists in europe have worked on a similar

Project to reintroduce Wolves into the Scottish highlands of

great Britain.

Edited Copy

Capitalization errors corrected (34 changes)

we had an opportunity to interview Author Simon Rush,

who was on Location in yellowstone Park doing Research

for his upcoming Book titled *The History of The gray Wolf*.

Rush explained that he had traveled throughout the west,

particularly in the rocky mountain states, with one

objective: to observe Wolves in their Native Habitat. Much

of his original information came from the international wolf

center (IWC), located in Ely, minnesota. Thanks to a

Relocation Project, many wolves have been moved to the

park, where they have thrived, feeding primarily on rabbits,

Deer, and Elk. scientists from all over the Earth have visited

yellowstone in recent years, not only to observe the Wolves,

but to assess their Impact on the Ecology of the Area. A

group of scientists in europe have worked on a similar

Project to reintroduce Wolves into the Scottish highlands of

great Britain.

Edited Copy

As it would appear in a publication

We had an opportunity to interview author Simon Rush,
who was on location in Yellowstone Park doing research for
his upcoming book titled *The History of the Gray Wolf*.
Rush explained that he had traveled throughout the West,
particularly in the Rocky Mountain states, with one
objective: to observe wolves in their native habitat. Much of
his original information came from the International Wolf
Center (IWC), located in Ely, Minnesota. Thanks to a
relocation project, many wolves have been moved to the
park, where they have thrived, feeding primarily on rabbits,
deer, and elk. Scientists from all over the earth have visited
Yellowstone in recent years, not only to observe the wolves,
but to assess their impact on the ecology of the area. A
group of scientists in Europe have worked on a similar
project to reintroduce wolves into the Scottish Highlands of
Great Britain.

Revising in Stages

Trait Connection: **Word Choice**

Introduction

Have you ever watched the same film more than once? If so, you may have noticed slightly different things the second time around—or the third. Revision is like that. The *best* writers will return to the same passage more than once because they know they're likely to see something on a return visit that they missed the first time. In this lesson, you'll revise twice. The first time, imagine yourself tidying up—as if clearing the clutter from a living room before guests come. Get rid of wordiness. Be ruthless about it. Shine a bright light on any tired words: *nice, good, special, wonderful*, etc. You know which ones they are. Replace them with something stronger—more vivid, more specific, more true to the moment. Then, take time to breathe. Read what you have written aloud, and try to see the scene in your mind. Ask yourself what is missing—what would give the piece that extra little something it needs to be memorable? The answer could be a "just right" descriptive word, an energetic verb, a comparison, or a sensory detail. Like adding a last-minute herb to the stew, add some zing to the writing.

Teacher's Sidebar . . .

The point of this lesson is to look—and then look again. Good revision is built upon this habit. This lesson focuses on word choice, but you can do layered revision based upon any trait. What makes this approach work is that students begin with what is *easier*— cutting wordiness and putting tired words to bed. Then, *with that done*, they tackle the more difficult task of saying precisely what they mean. To give this lesson real impact, allow a full day (or two) between Revision 1 and Revision 2. Students then see the midpoint draft with fresh eyes, and are likely to make more significant changes.

Focus and Intent

This lesson is intended to help students:

- Appreciate the power of two-step revision.
- Identify a series of word-choice-related revision tasks.
- Revise a passage in stages, looking for specific problems at each stage.

Teaching the Lesson

Step 1: Going Step by Step

Clearing the clutter helps you see the "bones" of your writing. Then you know whether you've actually said anything. In this part of the lesson, we'll exercise restraint. That means you don't need to take on *every* word choice issue at once, but only two: wordiness and use of tired words. Cut the number of words by at least a third—more if you can. Replace tired words and expressions with something stronger. Then step back to see (and hear) how it all looks. The first example is done for you.

1. A big, gigantic, angry lion leaped and bounded from the bushes, and stood before us, facing us head on, so close you couldn't believe it, and it was totally unbelievable. (31 words)

    Revision

    A lion bounded from the bushes, and stood facing us, so close you could smell the foulness of his breath. (20 words)

2. The colossal, bustling city sprawled in every direction, so massive, so intrusive on the landscape, we couldn't see to the end of it, and yet it was just amazing and special to be there taking in all the sights and sounds and smells of the city in all its glory. (51 words)

    Revision

    _____

    _____

3. One of the very most wonderful foods on earth is not what you might first think of, but the humble, tiny, seemingly inconsequential sunflower seed, which carries a surprising, amazing number of nutrients inside its small miniscule shell, and is actually, surprisingly enough, nutritious enough to keep a human being going for the longest time. (56 words)

    Revision

    _____

    _____

If you are thinking that our writing (like the city in Sample 2) grew sprawlier—and worse—as we went along, you were paying close attention. We went from 31 to 51 to 56 words. But—what about you? How much did you *cut?* What other word choices did you make? Choose one example—either 2 or 3—and rewrite it to create an indelible moment the reader cannot erase from his or her mind. A moment as striking as a painting on the wall. Here's our *revision* of *revision 1:*

Revision 2

Exploding from the bushes, the lion spewed his foul, steaming breath across our blood-drained faces. (15 words)

Step 2: Making the Reading-Writing Connection

In *Birdland*, by Tracy Mack, Jed and his best friend Flyer are making a documentary of their New York neighborhood. Finding the "just right" moments to film causes Jed and Flyer to notice the tiniest of details—and the vivid way in which those details are expressed almost makes us feel as if we're already watching the video:

Sample

Inside, the beautiful Melody floats from one end of the counter to the other. Her long amber curls bounce like Slinkies around her shining face, and the tiny diamond stud on the side of her nose glistens. When she sees us she smiles and waves one long, wand-like arm to motion us over.

(From *Birdland* by Tracy Mack. 2003. New York: Scholastic, p. 28.)

Let's try a little pop quiz to see how effective Tracy Mack's word choice in this passage really was. Can you recall the word Mack uses to describe how Melody moves from one end of the counter to the other? (*floats*) Mack compares Melody's long amber curls to something—what? (*Slinkies*) According to the passage, Melody's waving arm is not only long, but also . . . what? (*wand-like*) As you may have guessed, this is not only a quiz for you, but also for the author. When readers *remember* your words, you can be confident you chose well. How did Tracy Mack do with you and your fellow students?

Step 3: Involving Students as Evaluators

Ask students to review Samples A and B, looking and listening for word choice that is memorable. Which writer is more concise? Which avoids clichés and tired words? Which creates vivid moments likely to stay in the reader's memory? Encourage students to highlight moments that work—from either passage—and to cut what is not needed or revise any words or phrases with something stronger (in either passage).

Discussing Results

Most students should find Sample A stronger. It is both concise and vivid. The writer of Sample B, by contrast, is not only repetitive, but also settles for the first word or phrase that comes to mind. A first revision of Sample B, and a second revision building on the first, are provided as examples.

Step 4: Modeling Revision

- Share Sample C (*Whole Class Revision*) with students. Read it aloud.

- Ask whether the passage is wordy (most students should say *yes*) and whether the writer has a tendency to use tired words (most students should say *yes* to this also).

- Work through two revisions. *For Revision 1:* Cross out anything that can be cut. Ask students to guide you as you do this. Then, highlight any tired words or phrases and replace them with something fresh.

- *For Revision 2:* Read Revision 1 aloud, and ask students to look for *one moment* that they could bring to life with a vivid image, precise adjective, strong verb, or memorable sensory impression. Make that change—and read the second revision aloud, comparing it with the original.

- Compare your second draft with ours if you wish, keeping in mind that your revision need not match ours. What matters is the *contrast* between the original and your second draft.

Step 5: Revising with Partners

Share Sample D (*Revising with Partners*). Ask students to follow the basic steps you modeled with Sample C. *Working with partners,* they should:

- Read the passage aloud, looking and listening for wordiness and overused words or phrases.

- Cut any words that are repetitive or unneeded.

- Highlight overused words and revise them.

- Read their revisions aloud to hear the impact of their changes.

- *For more dramatic results, wait one to two days before doing Revision 2.*

- At this point (*Revision 2*), identify one moment that could be revised to create a vivid impression on the reader—and change it by creating a striking image or sensory detail, or including a strong adjective or verb.

- Compare their revisions with the original draft—and then with our revision (keeping in mind that their revisions need not match ours).

Step 6: Sharing and Discussing Results

When students have finished, ask several pairs of students to share their revisions by reading first Revision 1—and then Revision 2. Which teams made the most dramatic changes from the original to the first revision? From Revision 1 to Revision 2? Did second drafts differ more than first drafts? Why might this happen?

Next Steps

- Practice multi-leveled revision routinely—with any writing you do. If you are focusing on a particular trait, break it into features so that students can tackle one or two at a time. For example, with organization, you might revise for general order in one round, then fine tune the lead and conclusion in the next.

- Encourage students to write to any authors whose work they admire and ask about their revision process. How many times do their favorite writers revise before sending a draft to a publisher? How many times after the publisher first sees it? Talk about the difference between multiple revisions and "revision" as it is generally taught in school.

- Look and listen for samples of strong word choice in the literature you share aloud. Pay attention to strong imagery, good use of verbs to create energy and motion, a light touch with adjectives, and conciseness. Recommended:
  - *Birdland* by Tracy Mack. 2003. New York: Scholastic.
  - *The Adventures of Marco Polo* by Russell Freedman. 2006. New York: Scholastic.
  - *Living Up the Street* by Gary Soto. 1985. New York: Bantam Doubleday.
  - *A Northern Light* by Jennifer Donnelly. 2003. New York: Harcourt.

- *For an additional challenge:* Create a practice revision lesson by following the steps of this lesson in reverse. Begin with a passage you think is particularly strong. Replace any vivid words or phrases with something flat. Replace images with generalities. Add words—then add some more. Make copies in double- or triple-spaced print, and give them to students (in two-person teams) to revise in stages. See who can come closest to the author's original. By all means, let them know who the author is, for style influences word choice. Share students' revisions—and the author's original—with the rest of the class. How *daring* are you? For an even greater challenge, ask students to design a lesson like this for you—and share *your* revision!

Sample A: Inevitability

The ocean waited patiently for the sun, as it had done for millions of years. But the sun took its time, sliding down the curve of sky right on schedule, hurrying for no one. It took time to change the lighting from gold to lavender, time to touch every cloud that reached out a hand. In the end, though, even a major celebrity like the sun can hold out only just so long. It slipped quietly into the sea without so much as a round of applause. The sea, meanwhile, rolled on as if nothing spectacular had happened at all.

Sample B: Watch the Ears

A bull elephant can be a very dangerous and frightening animal. They are extremely intimidating. They are so big and awesome it takes your breath away. They look as if they cannot run fast, but that is actually a misperception. In fact, they are amazing runners. They can move like lightning, covering an enormous amount of ground with a single stride. In fact, they are so much faster than a human that running from them is really quite useless. There is one thing that saves a lot of people, however. Elephants have a special thing they like to do. They like to bluff. It takes a massive amount of energy for an elephant to run, so before wasting its valuable energy in a chase, an elephant will flap and wave its ears menacingly. That is the signal to retreat. If you see an elephant do this, do NOT ignore this signal. Back up slowly, gradually putting more and more distance between yourself and the elephant. Very likely, you will be safe.

(171 words)

Sample B, Revision #1

A bull elephant can be ~~a very dangerous and frightening animal. They are~~ extremely intimidating. ~~They are so big and awesome it takes your breath away.~~ They look as if they cannot run fast, but that is ~~actually a~~ [potentially dangerous] misperception. In fact, [elephants] ~~they are amazing runners. They~~ can move like lightning, covering [up to 40 feet] ~~an enormous amount of ground~~ with a single stride. ~~In fact, they are so much faster than a human that~~ Running from them is ~~really quite~~ useless. ~~There is one thing that saves a lot of people, however.~~ Elephants ~~have a special thing they like to do. They~~ like to bluff. [however.] ~~It takes a massive amount of energy for an elephant to run, so~~ Before wasting its valuable energy in a chase, an elephant will flap ~~and wave~~ its ears menacingly. That is the signal to retreat. ~~If you see an elephant do this, do NOT~~ [NEVER] ignore this signal. Back up slowly, ~~gradually putting more and more distance between yourself and the elephant. Very~~ [and with luck,] ~~likely~~ you will be safe.

Sample B, Revision #2

A bull elephant can be ~~extremely~~ *disarmingly* intimidating. They look as

are slow and lumbering,

if they ~~cannot run fast~~ but that is a potentially dangerous

misperception. In fact, ~~elephants can move like lightning~~

because even an old, tired elephant can cover more ground with a single stride than the most agile human athlete can cover in ten,

~~covering up to 40 feet with a single stride~~ running from

Like most poker players, however, elephants enjoy a good

them is useless. ~~Elephants like to~~ bluff ⊙ ~~however~~ Before

wasting its valuable energy in a chase, an elephant will flap

its ears menacingly. That is the signal to retreat. NEVER

Even if you are armed, the elephant holds better cards.   *if you can convince the elephant he's won the game,*

ignore this signal. Back up slowly, and ~~with luck~~ you will

be safe.

(120 words)

Sample C: Whole Class Revision

Freedom Riders

In the early 1960s, 1961 to be exact, a group of incredibly brave and courageous college students got together and boarded a bus in Tennessee. They headed away from their homes and into the deep South. They were not intending to break any laws, or do anything illegal, but they were definitely breaking with a long-standing tradition and that was what made this group of Freedom Riders, as they called themselves, so special. The students were both black and white, and though it wasn't universally accepted at that time, they intended to travel together, sit together, and eat together in a time when many people did not believe in crossing racial lines in this way. They were met with much resistance and violence. People who favored segregation shouted insults at the Freedom Riders. They were attacked and beaten. But, inspired by the teachings of Dr. Martin Luther King, Jr., they were determined to respond only in totally nonviolent ways. With awesome and inspiring determination, they refused to attack their attackers, enduring even the most brutal and outrageous violence without retaliation. Their courage inspired generations of students to fight for civil rights.

(191 words)

Sample D: Revising with Partners

Marco Polo

Of all the explorers in the world, one of the most famous and interesting has got to be the famous Marco Polo. This incredible and fascinating man lived in the thirteenth century in the city of Venice, which is located in Italy. People in Marco Polo's family were traders and merchants for the most part, so it is not surprising that from an early age, Marco Polo longed to travel and explore. He claimed to have made an amazing and wonderful journey across Asia to the court of the Chinese ruler Kublai Khan, and he wrote a book about his amazing, mind-blowing adventures. The book was titled *The Description of the World*. In this special book, he claimed to have seen many remarkable things, including mountains so high birds could not fly over them. Many readers believed he was exaggerating and making up his unbelievable tales. Perhaps we will never know the truth for sure.

(155 words)

Suggested Revisions of C and D

Sample C: Whole Class Revision
Revision #1

Freedom Riders

In ~~the early 1960s,~~ 1961 ~~to be exact,~~ a group of ~~incredibly~~ **brave** ~~and courageous~~ college students ~~got together and~~ boarded a bus in Tennessee. ~~They headed away from their homes and~~ **and headed** into the deep South. **Though** they were not ~~intending to break~~ **breaking** any laws, ~~or do anything illegal,~~ ~~but~~ they were definitely breaking with a long-standing tradition (of racial segregation,) and that was what made this group of Freedom Riders ~~as they called themselves~~ **unique.** ~~so special.~~ The students were both black and white, and though it wasn't universally accepted at that time, they intended to travel together, sit together, and eat together. ~~in a time when many people did not believe~~ ~~in crossing racial lines in this way.~~ They were met with ~~much resistance~~ (outrage from segregationists, who) ~~and violence. People who favored segregation~~ shouted insults at the Freedom Riders. They were attacked and beaten. But, inspired by the teachings of Dr. Martin Luther King, Jr., ~~they were determined to respond only in totally nonviolent ways. With awesome and inspiring~~ ~~determination~~ they refused to ~~attack~~ **turn on** their attackers, enduring even the most brutal ~~and outrageous~~ violence without retaliation. Their courage inspired generations of students to fight for civil rights.

(128 words)

Sample C: Whole Class Revision
Revision #2

Freedom Riders

In 1961 a brave group college students boarded a bus in Tennessee and headed into the deep South. Though they were not breaking any laws, they were definitely breaking with a long-standing tradition of racial segregation, and that made this group of Freedom Riders unique. The **knowing fully that** students were both black and white, and ~~though~~ it wasn't universally accepted at that time, they intended to travel together, sit together, and eat together. They were met with outrage from segregationists, who **screamed insults, attacked them with dogs, and beat them with clubs.** ~~shouted insults at the Freedom Riders. They were attacked and beaten.~~

But, inspired by the teachings of Dr. Martin Luther King, Jr., ~~they~~ **the Freedom Riders refused to strike one blow in retaliation.** ~~refused to turn on their attackers, enduring even the most brutal violence~~ **awakened the conscience of a nation, inspiring** ~~without retaliation.~~ Their courage ~~inspired~~ generations of students to **demand** ~~fight for~~ civil rights, **and to rethink the power of passive resistance.**

(138 words)

Sample D: Revising with Partners
Marco Polo, Revision #1

Marco Polo

Among ~~Of all the explorers in the world, one of~~ the most ~~famous and~~ interesting

explorers is ~~has got to be~~ the ~~famous~~ Marco Polo. *daring* ~~This incredible and fascinating~~

who ~~man~~ lived in ~~the~~ thirteenth century ~~in the city of~~ Venice, ~~which is~~

Born into a family of ~~located in Italy. People in Marco Polo's family were~~ traders and

merchants, ~~for the most part, so it is not surprising that from an early~~

~~age,~~ Marco Polo longed to travel and explore (from the time he was a young boy.) He claimed to have made

arduous but exciting
an ~~amazing and wonderful~~ journey across Asia to the court of the

Chinese ruler Kublai Khan, and he wrote a book about his ~~amazing~~

~~mind-blowing~~ adventures. ~~The book was~~ titled *The Description of the*

World. In this ~~special~~ book, he claimed to have seen many remarkable

things, including mountains so high birds could not fly over them. Many

readers believed he was exaggerating, ~~and making up his unbelievable~~

~~tales.~~ Perhaps we will never know ~~the truth~~ for sure.

Sample D: Revising with Partners
Marco Polo, Revision #2

Marco Polo

Among the most interesting explorers is the daring Marco Polo, who

lived in thirteenth century Venice. Born into a family of traders and

merchants, Marco Polo longed ~~to travel and explore~~ from the time he

(to explore the world. His dream came true, apparently, when he)

was a young boy. ~~He claimed to have~~ made an arduous but exciting

journey across Asia to the court of the Chinese ruler Kublai Khan. ~~and~~

later
He wrote a book about his adventures titled *The Description of the*

(Though the title was less than fascinating, the book made
remarkable claims—or at least they were remarkable in
the 1200s. For example, Polo declared he had seen)

World. ~~In this book, he claimed to have seen many remarkable things~~

~~including~~ mountains so high birds could not fly over them. ~~Many readers~~

(Today, we take such tales in stride, but thirteenth century readers felt sure)
~~believed~~ he was exaggerating. Perhaps ~~we will never know for sure~~

he was—or perhaps those readers were just jealous that Polo got

to see the world for himself.

(147 words)

More on Capitals

Trait Connection: **Conventions**

Introduction (Share with students in your own words—or as a handout.)

Rules governing use of capitals sometimes seem endless, but for the most part, they follow common sense. Remember, capital letters are big and bold; they're designed to get attention. So, use them to mark names, acronyms, and titles. Here are some examples just a little different from those you encountered in the preceding lesson on capitals. Capitalize:

- A word like *Aunt, Uncle, Mom*, or *Dad* when used *as a name*: **As you can see, Uncle Bill loves bowling. So does Dad.** (But—**Bill is my uncle. My dad loves to bowl.**)

- Letters that are part of a term: **My mom has a V-shaped T-shirt.**

- Names of teams or organizations: **He belongs to the Latin Club, 4-H, the Highland Park Wildcats, and Young Democrats of America.**

- Titles of specific courses (but *not* fields of study): **Judy is taking Psychology 101 this term.** (But—**Judy is studying psychology.**)

- Acronyms: **The Food and Drug Administration (FDA) has many rules governing the labeling of foods.**

- The words *freshman, sophomore, junior* and *senior* ONLY when they are used as part of a name or term: **We attended the Freshman Orientation Program.** (But—**Julie is a freshman this year.**)

It's about names—and specifics. Even the best editors have questions from time to time, though, so as you go through this lesson, be sure you have a handbook to which you can refer—and be sure you can find examples of correctly used capitals. As a reminder, you can change a lower case letter to a capital in one of two ways: Draw a triple underscore beneath the letter that should be capitalized, or draw a caret right into the letter and print the capital above it, like this:

joellen will not be taking introduction to biology this term.

When a word is capitalized, but should *not* be, draw a slash mark through the capital, like this:

Instead, she will take another Science Course—I'm not sure which one.

Teaching the Lesson (General Guidelines for Teachers)

1. Share the examples above, or make up your own examples to acquaint students with additional rules involving capitals.

2. Make sure everyone understands how to edit capitalization errors, whether it's a missing capital or a capital that should not be there.

3. Make sure students have access to a good handbook (*Write Source: The New Generation* published by Great Source Education is recommended) to which they can refer during the lesson.

4. Remind students to read the passage aloud, asking as they go, "Is this reference being used as a proper name or a common noun?" Also remind them to look for missing capitals as well as capitals that are *not needed*.

5. Share the editing lesson on the following page. Ask students to read the text aloud, looking and listening for capitalization errors.

6. Ask students to edit individually first, then check with a partner.

7. When everyone is done, ask them to coach you as you edit the same copy.

8. When you finish, read your edited copy aloud, talking about the reasons behind each change; then compare your edited copy with our suggested text on page 193.

Editing Goal: Catch and correct 41 capitalization errors.
(See Editor's Note on "Internet," following Edited Copy.
Also note that each change counts as one error.)
Follow-Up: Watch for capitalization errors in your own work.

Editing Practice

Correct all capitalization errors.

Mr. Lee, who teaches biology II, is a member of nrdc (the natural resources defense council) as well as Peta (people for the ethical treatment of animals). He has taught Biology (as well as Chemistry) now for more than Twenty Years, and has recently been invited by Freeport college to develop an Online Science Course relating to Ecological Studies. The course will be designed for people working on a B.A. (bachelor of arts) Degree, and will be taught entirely over the Internet. Thus far, mr. lee has the full support of the World Wildlife Fund (wwf), and several other Conservation and Wildlife Organizations. He is hopeful that his Course will be fully accredited so that students can transfer their three credits to the local State University programs in either Biology or Ecology. As a lifelong Environmentalist, Mr. lee takes particular satisfaction in this Lifetime Achievement—which has reportedly even garnered some attention from greenpeace international.

Edited Copy

Capitalization errors corrected (41 changes)

Mr. Lee, who teaches biology II, is a member of nrdc (the natural resources defense council) as well as Peta (people for the ethical treatment of animals). He has taught Biology (as well as Chemistry) now for more than Twenty Years, and has recently been invited by Freeport college to develop an Online Science Course relating to Ecological Studies. The course will be designed for people working on a B.A. (bachelor of arts) Degree, and will be taught entirely over the Internet. Thus far, mr. lee has the full support of the World Wildlife Fund (wwf), and several other Conservation and Wildlife Organizations. He is hopeful that his Course will be fully accredited so that students can transfer their three credits to the local State University programs in either Biology or Ecology. As a lifelong Environmentalist, Mr. lee takes particular satisfaction in this Lifetime Achievement—which has reportedly even garnered some attention from greenpeace international.

Editor's Note
The *New York Times* and other well-known American publications routinely capitalize "Internet." It appears in lower case form, however, in some publications, and is often so used informally, as in e-mail. The debate goes on—and many handbooks do not include it because it is controversial. Take a class vote!

Revising for Accuracy

Trait Connection: **Word Choice**

Introduction

Maybe you've been in a situation where you're reaching for the right word, but . . . it just *won't come to you*. What do you do? Some writers think of a synonym and look it up, hoping to pinpoint the very word they were looking for. But if you're in a hurry, you might not take time to do that. You might just reach for a word you think—and hope—will do. In conversation, this often works out because after all, you're right there to clarify any misunderstanding. In writing, though, the use of a word that's even a little off-target can distort meaning—sometimes in humorous ways, often in confusing ways. In this lesson, you'll look and listen for incorrect use of words, and revise for accuracy by finding a replacement for each word used incorrectly.

Teacher's Sidebar . . .

Students will need access to a dictionary and/or thesaurus for this lesson. In the warm-up, questionable words are underlined. Later, students must judge for themselves whether words in practice revision passages are used correctly. In each case, only two or three words are misused, but students will need to determine which those are.

Focus and Intent

This lesson is intended to help students:

- Recognize the importance of using words accurately.
- Distinguish between words that are used correctly and words that do not fit the writer's intended meaning.
- Revise a passage by replacing incorrectly used words with suitable substitutes.

Teaching the Lesson

Step 1: Watching for Misfits

In some of the following passages, the **boldfaced** word is used correctly. In others, it does not fit the writer's intended meaning. You must first determine what the writer is intending to say; only then can you judge whether a word is being used correctly. If you are not sure of a word's meaning, by all means, look it up. Good writers work with a dictionary and thesaurus in reach. Cross out any word that is misused, and replace it with a better choice.

1. The hunters made a **sodden** move, scaring the deer out of the brush.

2. We could not be sure if he was telling the truth about the shoplifting incident until a witness **collaborated** his story.

3. The **artifice** of the building was breathtakingly beautiful.

4. The pirates, unfortunately, were in **collusion** with the authorities.

5. Misappropriation of funds can lead to a financial **debacle**.

Note: Boldfaced words in sentences 4 and 5 are used correctly. In sentences 1, 2, and 3, the correct words should be *sudden*, *corroborated*, and *façade*, respectively. *Sodden* means *soggy*; *collaborated* means *worked together*; and *artifice* means *ruse* or *pretense*. Keep in mind that this warm-up is a bit easier than the actual revision to come because the words in question are identified.

Step 2: Making the Reading-Writing Connection

Mary Shelley was only 18 when she began writing *Frankenstein*, a book first published anonymously in 1818, then in a revised edition in 1831. *Frankenstein*, often regarded as an ancestor of the horror genre (though also a romance and book of philosophy), was written nearly two hundred years ago; and this certainly accounts, in part, for a style and syntax very different from what we would expect in contemporary writing. Still, it is difficult not to be struck by Mary Shelley's extraordinary vocabulary. Here is a sampling of words from one short passage: *utter, incoherent, self-reproach, resolution, tempest, repentance, superfluous, heed, remorse, diabolical, vengeance, extremity*. How many are familiar to you? Would you know whether each word was used well—or incorrectly? Following is the passage from which these words are taken—a passage in which the speaker is confronting Dr. Frankenstein's monster:

Sample

The monster continued to utter wild and incoherent self-reproaches. At length I gathered resolution to address him in a pause of the tempest of his passion: "Your repentance," I said, "is now superfluous. If you had listened to the voice of conscience, and heeded the stings of remorse, before you had urged your diabolical vengeance to this extremity, Frankenstein would yet have lived."

(From *Frankenstein* by Mary Shelley. 2003. New York: Barnes & Noble Classics, p. 216.)

Do these words strike you as the "just right" choices for this passage? Would you change any of them? Actually—even though Shelley's words are absolutely used correctly—you probably *would* say things differently. For a challenge, try translating Shelley's prose into modern vernacular.

Step 3: Involving Students as Evaluators

Ask students to review Samples A and B, looking and listening for words that are used incorrectly. For this practice, no particular words are identified for consideration. Students must be careful readers, attending to each writer's meaning, and asking whether the chosen words support that meaning. Have students work with a partner, highlighting words that they feel are used incorrectly and making marginal notes about possible substitutes. Encourage students to use a dictionary or thesaurus to explore the meaning of any words—whether they feel they know them already or not.

Discussing Results

Most students should find Sample A stronger. The writer uses words clearly and correctly. Writer B, by contrast, misuses several words—though the intent is fairly clear. Discuss differences between the two pieces, asking students to identify words they feel are used incorrectly, and having them brainstorm alternatives. One possible revision of Sample B is provided.

Step 4: Modeling Revision

- Share Sample C (*Whole Class Revision*) with students. Read it aloud.

- Ask whether this writer uses words correctly—or whether some word choices could leave readers confused. (Most students should say *confused.*)

- Identify any word or words that should be replaced.

- Look the words up in a dictionary and/or thesaurus and discuss possible alternatives. Try several by reading the sentence aloud, and choosing the alternative that works best.

- Revise by replacing any incorrectly used words.

- Compare your draft with ours if you wish, keeping in mind that your revision need not match ours—so long as you choose an alternate word or expression with meaning that reflects the writer's intent.

Step 5: Revising with Partners

Share Sample D (*Revising with Partners*). Ask students to follow the basic steps you modeled with Sample C. *Working with partners,* they should:

- Read the passage aloud, looking and listening for words that are used incorrectly.

- Highlight any words that should be replaced.

- Look up each word they plan to replace in the dictionary and/or thesaurus, exploring the meaning and connotations, and thinking about which alternative best captures the writer's intended meaning.

- Revise by replacing each incorrectly used word with the best possible alternative. It is fine to *revise a whole phrase or reword a sentence.*
- Read their revisions aloud to hear the impact of their changes.
- Compare their revisions with ours, keeping in mind that their revisions need not match ours in any way.

Step 6: Sharing and Discussing Results

When students have finished, ask several pairs of students to share their revised passages aloud. Which teams chose the words that best reflect the writer's meaning? When more than one substitution is possible, how does a good writer make the choice?

Next Steps

- As any good thesaurus shows, a writer *may* have a number of possible alternatives for any given word. When this is the case, how does he or she make a choice? List possible synonyms for one or two words, and talk about differences in connotation. Consider how word choice influences not only literal meaning, but also mood and imagery.

- Ask students to review their own writing, highlighting any words about which they feel unsure—or for which they feel there could be a better alternative. Ask them to share these words in response groups, where teams can work together to brainstorm or research good alternatives.

- Watch and listen for new or particularly well-used words in the literature you share aloud. Recommended:
  - *Frankenstein* by Mary Shelley. 2003. New York: Barnes & Noble Classics.
  - *In My Hands: Memories of a Holocaust Rescuer* by Irene Gut Opdyke. 1999. New York: Random House.
  - *A Northern Light* by Jennifer Donnelly. 2004. New York: Harcourt.
  - *The Schwa Was Here* by Neal Schusterman. 2004. New York: Puffin.

- *For an additional challenge:* Students may have already tried revising the Mary Shelley passage from the *Reading-Writing Connection* by translating it into contemporary vernacular. If not, invite them to do so—and to compare their translations (which tend to take on the voice of the translator). Take the translation challenge with various other passages from Shelley's book—or *any* piece of writing with a publication date preceding 1900.

Sample A

Personality Plus—or Minus?

Irene had an effervescent personality. She was

loquacious, always looking for a new topic of conversation.

By contrast, her friend Hannah was reticent—almost shy, in

fact. She considered Irene a bit brash, but unobtrusive

people often have a more conservative perspective. Truth be

told, Irene was just an extrovert, plain and simple. She had

been gregarious since childhood. "I like to think I'm

assertive—but not aggressive," she was fond of saying.

"Irene's a live wire," her grandfather said. He

enjoyed her conviviality, and didn't mind.

Hannah would have preferred a more retiring sort of

friend, but she was never disparaging about Irene. She felt

derogatory remarks were uncalled for. Maybe there was

some truth to the old saying that "opposites attract."

Sample B

Words misused? Stronger possibilities?

The Match

I approached the mat, eyeing the referee haphazardly, staring mostly at my opponent. He was staring back, trying hard to bluff me into thinking he was more inept than he was. From the way he was standing, I was convinced he was experienced, and knew what he was doing. The ref blew his whistle, and we went at it. I fell on my knees, grabbed his legs, and made a weak, prophetic attempt at a take-down. He wrapped a muscular forearm around my head and neck, and I could feel adrenaline crush through my veins. I reached up in a desperate attempt to throw him off balance, but he was too cursory for me, and before I knew what was happening, I was flat on my back, staring up into blinding overhead lights.

Revision of Sample B

The Match

I approached the mat, eyeing the referee ~~haphazardly~~ distractedly, staring

mostly at my opponent. He was staring back, trying hard to

bluff me into thinking he was more ~~inept~~ adept than he was. From the

way he was standing, I was convinced he was experienced, and

knew what he was doing. The ref blew his whistle, and we went

at it. I fell on my knees, grabbed his legs, and made a weak,

~~prophetic~~ pathetic attempt at a take-down. He wrapped a muscular

forearm around my head and neck, and I could feel adrenaline

~~crush~~ course through my veins. I reached up in a desperate attempt to

throw him off balance, but he was too ~~cursory~~ fast for me, and

before I knew what was happening, I was flat on my back,

staring up into blinding overhead lights.

Other possibilities:
distractedly: *inattentively, in an unfocused way*
adept: *skillful, practiced, proficient, adroit*
pathetic: *feeble, meager*
course: *rush, flow, gush, tear*
fast: *quick, speedy*

Sample C: Whole Class Revision

Words misused? Stronger possibilities?

Conflict

My sister, who is 15, feels she is old enough to date. My parents could not be in greater apposition. Emily, for her part, says their values are antiqued and outmoded. She has impelled them to listen, but they won't. Still, Emily is the most tenacious, irresolute person I have ever known. Once she makes up her mind, you might as well sit back for the duration of the contest. She will not budge.

Frankly, I don't know what the big deal is. Before you can *have* a date, you have to be *asked* on a date. I don't claim to be psychic or anything, but I don't teleport any romantic involvement in Emily's immediate future. So— why get all distressed? By the time she is asked out, both Emily and my parents will be massively older.

Sample D: Revising with Partners

Maasai People: Brave Nomads of Kenya

The Maasai live in a dry, aromatic part of northern Kenya, in Africa. They are nomads, moving with their animals to find grazing land and water. To the Maasai, animals are highly valuable, and are slaughtered only for special occasions. The Maasai rarely eat meat, but they do drink the milk and blood from their animals. Maasai children as young as five or six are inured with the care of young animals, in order to learn responsibility. The primary concern is protecting herds from risks, such as lions. To protect their animals, the Maasai rely on their nomadic lifestyle, on thorny fences that surround herds at night— and of course, on gruesome courage. Every Maasai warrior must, at some time, face down a lion. That is a task requiring real impudence.

Note
Information for this passage is based, in part, on *Facing the Lion: Growing Up Maasai in the African Savannah* by Joseph Lemasolai Lekuton. 2003. Washington, DC: National Geographic.

Suggested Revisions of C and D

Sample C: Whole Class Revision

Conflict

My sister, who is 15, feels she is old enough to date. My

parents could not be in greater ~~apposition~~ *opposition.* Emily, for her

part, says their values are ~~antiqued~~ *antiquated* and outmoded. She has

~~impelled~~ *implored* them to listen, but they won't. Still, Emily is the

most tenacious, ~~irresolute~~ *resolute* person I have ever known. Once

she makes up her mind, you might as well sit back for the

duration of the contest. She will not budge.

Frankly, I don't know what the big deal is. Before

you can *have* a date, you have to be *asked* on a date. I don't

claim to be psychic or anything, but I don't ~~teleport~~ *foresee* any

romantic involvement in Emily's immediate future. So—

why get all ~~distressed?~~ *stressed?* By the time she is asked out, both

Emily and my parents will be ~~massively~~ *considerably* older.

Alternatives:

be in greater opposition: *disagree more, feel a greater sense of conflict,*
   feel more hostile to the idea, be more resistant
antiquated: *outdated, outmoded, antediluvian, old-fashioned*
implored: *beseeched, pleaded*
resolute: *determined, unflinching, strong-minded, unwavering*
foresee: *predict, envision, imagine*
stressed: *worried, anxious, frazzled, jittery*
considerably: *much, far, a great deal*

Sample D: Revising with Partners

Maasai People: Brave Nomads of Kenya

The Maasai live in a dry, ~~aromatic~~ part of northern Kenya, in [arid]

Africa. They are nomads, moving with their animals to find

grazing land and water. To the Maasai, animals are highly

valuable, and are slaughtered only for special occasions. The

Maasai rarely eat meat, but they do drink the milk and blood from

their animals. Maasai children as young as five or six are ~~inured~~ [entrusted]

with the care of young animals, in order to learn responsibility.

The primary concern is protecting herds from ~~risks,~~ such as lions. [predators,]

To protect their animals, the Maasai rely on their nomadic

lifestyle, on thorny fences that surround herds at night—and of

course, on ~~gruesome~~ courage. Every Maasai warrior must, at [incredible]

some time, face down a lion. That is a task requiring real

~~impudence.~~ [valor.]

Alternatives:
arid: *parched, scorched, barren*
entrusted: *trusted*
predators: *killers, marauders*
incredible: *remarkable, striking, inspiring, awesome*
valor: *bravery, spirit, nerve, heroism, boldness (You do not want to repeat "courage")*

Putting It All Together
(Editing Lessons 18, 20, and 22)

Lesson 24

Trait Connection: **Conventions**

Introduction (Share with students in your own words—or as a handout.)

In this lesson, you will have a chance to put skills from three editing lessons together. Warm up with the following three examples. Answers appear at the end of this introduction.

- Insert capitals that the writer has forgotten:

  Ralph and bernie were headed for the san juan islands, going west through montana, and across the rocky mountains into the Pacific northwest.

- Delete capitals that do not belong:

  Alice was thinking of becoming a Nurse, but low grades in Chemistry and Biology made her apprehensive about getting into a good University.

- Put modifiers in their place:

  The waiter approached the table where we sat carrying some menus and water glasses.

Teaching the Lesson (General Guidelines for Teachers)

1. Begin by reviewing any information covered in Lessons 18, 20, and 22 about which students may have questions.
2. Practice editing using the samples above, or create your own.
3. Encourage students to refer to Lessons 18, 20, and 22 as they work on Lesson 24. We recommend making handbooks available: e.g., *Write Source: The New Generation*.

4. Share the editing lesson on the following page. Students should read the passage aloud, looking *and listening* for misplaced modifiers, and watching for missing or inappropriate capitals.

5. Ask them to work individually first, then check with a partner.

6. When everyone is done, ask them to coach you as you edit the same copy, making any changes you and they decide are important. When you finish, compare your edited copy to the one on page 208.

Edited Copy for Warm-Up Sentences

- Insert capitals that the writer has forgotten:

    Ralph and bernie were headed for the san juan islands, going west through montana, and across the rocky mountains into the Pacific northwest.

- Delete capitals that do not belong:

    Alice was thinking of becoming a Nurse, but low grades in Chemistry and Biology made her apprehensive about getting into a good University.

- Put modifiers in their place:

    The waiter approached the table where we sat carrying some menus and water glasses.

Editing Practice

Edit sentences to eliminate misplaced modifiers.
Insert missing capitals, and eliminate inappropriate capitals.

As a member of aaa, it was always helpful to receive road maps when Steve Johnston and his family traveled throughout the u.s. Though he was a good Navigator, Steve was delighted to receive a Global Positioning System (gps) for his Birthday on july 17. As he knew well, the gps system operates 24 hours a day, seven days a week—and is extremely accurate. He felt confident that he could find any location with satellite-based Technology. The Johnston Family put their new System to the test traveling from southern California to the everglades in Florida. The system did its job well, as the family sat there comfortably, announcing every city and turn just at the right time. They didn't even have to open one map! Talking about the trip later, the Navigation System only let them make one wrong turn—somewhere on the Plains of Texas—and that was only because they failed to follow the gps instructions.

Edited Copy

20 corrections

As a member of aaa, ~~it was always~~ helpful to receive road maps when

Steve Johnston always found it

he

~~Steve Johnston~~ and his family traveled throughout the u.s. Though he

was a good Navigator, Steve was delighted to receive a Global

Positioning System (gps) for his Birthday on july 17. As he knew well,

the gps system operates 24 hours a day, seven days a week—and is

extremely accurate. He felt confident that he could find any location

with satellite-based Technology. The Johnston Family put their new

System to the test traveling from southern California to the everglades in

Florida. The system did its job well, as the family sat there comfortably,

announcing every city and turn just at the right time. They didn't even

Steve remarked that

have to open one map! Talking about the trip later, the Navigation

System only let them make one wrong turn—somewhere on the Plains

of Texas—and that was only because they failed to follow the gps

instructions.

Revising to Break Old Habits

Trait Connection: **Sentence Fluency**

Introduction

Little words like *and, but, so, then*, and *because* are incredibly helpful. They can link ideas in meaningful ways: *Jim felt tired* **and** *ready to quit,* **but** *he didn't* **because** *he knew his team was counting on him.* In the sentence you just read, these little words serve a useful purpose; they show how various ideas within the sentence are connected. Sometimes, however, writers get lazy. They use small connecting words by habit, stringing ideas together without bothering to show the true connections: *It was a beautifully sunny morning* **so** *Jake and Lily went for a hike* **because** *they wanted to meet some friends* **so then** *they hit the beach about 10 o'clock* **and** . . . In this "sentence," the little words do show how the ideas relate; they simply keep the writer from having to use a period and think of a new way to begin the next sentence. This is writing by habit—and it's a habit you do not want to hold onto. Does this mean you must erase *every* small connecting word from your writing? Not at all. It simply means that you should pay attention to how often you use these small words—and be sure you are using them *only* where they're needed.

Teacher's Sidebar . . .

In this lesson, make sure students understand that it is not the small linking words that are "evil." Writing by habit is using these words to suggest potentially misleading relationships between ideas. Make sure each student has a highlighter to mark small linking words. Making linking words stand out makes it easier to ask, "Is this word vital in creating a connection—or should it go?"

Focus and Intent

This lesson is intended to help students:

- Become more conscious of small linking words that connect ideas.
- Distinguish between purposeful use of linking words and writing by habit.
- Revise a passage by deleting unneeded linking words and finding more creative ways to begin sentences.

Teaching the Lesson

Step 1: Breaking the Habit

In the following passages, small connecting words are overused—mindlessly joining ideas without showing how they are truly related. Begin by highlighting the connecting words. Then revise by eliminating as many as you can (keep those you feel are critical) and rewriting to show the true connection between ideas. As you work, think of creative ways to begin sentences. Add any words you wish. The first example is done for you. (*Note: If you wind up with more than one sentence—and you should—try to make each new sentence begin a different way.*)

1. Jason was a little nervous **because** it was his first time diving **but** he was determined to go through with it, **so** he put on his wetsuit **and** grabbed his gear **and then** before he knew it he was headed out toward the red flag **because** that marked the spot where the group would begin their dive.

   Revision

   Because it was his first time diving, Jason felt more than a little nervous. He was determined to go through with it, however. Trying hard to control his shaking, he put on his wetsuit and grabbed his gear. The next thing he knew, he was headed out toward the red flag. That innocent looking piece of cloth marked the spot where the group would begin their dive.

2. E-mail is a way of sending messages electronically, so the word is really short for "electronic mail," and it can be a noun or verb, but although some people say it is fine to write "email" without the hyphen, and they think *e-mail* is out of date, many major usage manuals suggest retaining the hyphen, so it is probably good practice to do that for now.

   Revision

   _____

   _____

3. Most people have heard of smog which is a mixture of smoke and fog and this is where the name comes from, but not everyone has heard of "vog," and though it is similar to smog but because it is a combination of fog and volcanic dust, any place that has active volcanoes that shoot dust into the air might experience vog, because then it creates a low lying thick cloud with volcanic dust mixed into it and it can greatly reduce visibility.

   Revision

   _____

   _____

Step 2: Making the Reading-Writing Connection

In his passionate foreword to the book *Freedom Riders*, Congressman John Lewis urges readers to embark on their own personal journeys of civil justice and change. Notice how his avoidance of mindless connecting words combines with varied sentence beginnings to give his message momentum and power:

Sample

Our country needs you. It needs your drive, your dedication, your creativity, your ideas. Whatever it is you care about—whether it is saving the environment, world peace, equal justice under the law, or accessible health care—find your passion and make a difference. You, too can bring about a revolution of values, a revolution of ideas that can help this nation meet its highest destiny. You can change the world.

(From *Freedom Riders* by Ann Bausum. 2006. Washington, D. C.: National Geographic Society, p. 7.)

Imagine if John Lewis had written this heartfelt passage as one long "sentence," linking ideas with *and, so*, or *because*. Try it—then read the result aloud to hear just how diluted the message becomes.

Step 3: Involving Students as Evaluators

Ask students to review Samples A and B, looking and listening for small connecting words that are not actually needed—and may even suggest links between ideas that do not exist. Encourage students to work in teams, with highlighters in their hands, marking each connecting word and discussing whether it is helpful—or just mindless "writing by habit." Encourage them to also make marginal notes about how ideas are actually connected.

Discussing Results

Most students should find Sample A stronger. The writer uses small connecting words occasionally—but does so with purpose. By contrast, writer B creates a stream-of-consciousness "sentence," in which true relationships are fuzzy at best. Talk about differences between the two pieces. Also discuss which connecting words should be deleted from Sample B and replaced with language clarifying links between ideas. One possible revision of Sample B is provided.

Step 4: Modeling Revision

- Share Sample C (*Whole Class Revision*) with students. Read it aloud.
- Ask whether this writer uses connecting words to show actual relationships between ideas, or simply inserts them mindlessly to avoid beginning a new sentence. (Most students should say *inserts them mindlessly*.)
- Identify all small connecting words, and discuss whether each is vital or should be cut.
- Cut those that can go.

- Revise by creating new sentence beginnings that clarify connections. Feel free to flip sentences, cut anything, or add new words or phrases so that the piece reads smoothly. If possible, make *each new sentence* begin in a different way. (You can check this by underlining the first four words of each sentence when you finish.)

- Compare your draft with ours if you wish, keeping in mind that your revision need not match ours—so long as you got rid of mindless connecting words and found creative ways to link ideas.

Step 5: Revising with Partners

Share Sample D (*Revising with Partners*). Ask students to follow the basic steps you modeled with Sample C. *Working with partners,* they should:

- Read the passage aloud, looking and listening for small connecting words that the writer has included out of habit.

- Highlight all such words—and discuss which ones should be replaced.

- Cut unneeded linking words.

- Revise by writing new sentences that make connections between ideas clear. Try to begin each new sentence in a different way.

- Read their revisions aloud to hear the impact of their changes.

- Compare their revisions with ours, keeping in mind that their revisions need not match ours.

Step 6: Sharing and Discussing Results

When students have finished, ask several pairs of students to share their revised passages aloud. Do they sound very different? Notice that there is no "one right way" to link ideas.

Next Steps

- How many different ways are there to write a given sentence? Try it and find out. Rewrite the following sentence as many ways as you can within two minutes. (You should come up with *at least* 10—and if you think of 20, that's terrific!)

  Strong writers always find creative ways to begin sentences.

- Ask students to review their own writing, looking for those pesky connecting words that are only included out of habit. Ask them to delete as many as they can, and revise by finding ways to connect ideas more clearly and vary sentence beginnings.

■ Watch and listen for carefully crafted, varied sentences in the literature you share aloud. Notice—and applaud—writers who do not overuse mindless connecting words. Recommended:

- *Freedom Riders* by Ann Bausum. 2006. Washington, DC: National Geographic Society.

- *Escape! The Story of the Great Houdini* by Sid Fleischman. 2006. New York: HarperCollins.

- *Quest for the Tree Kangaroo* by Sy Montgomery. 2006. Boston: Houghton Mifflin.

- *Who Was First? Discovering the Americas* by Russell Freedman. 2007. Boston: Houghton Mifflin.

■ *For an additional challenge:* Students may have already tried revising the John Lewis passage from the *Reading-Writing Connection* by turning it into one long "sentence" with phrases or clauses linked by small connecting words. Invite them to try this with any other passage of their choice. (Check the recommended books for examples.) Begin with something well written; then rewrite it as if everything had to be crammed into one endless "sentence." Revisions should be double spaced. When students have finished this exercise, ask them to trade "monster sentences" with partners and revise again, this time *eliminating* the connecting words. Compare these revisions to the authors' originals.

Sample A

and, but, so, because:
Overused?
Clear connections?
Varied beginnings?

Giant Travelers

When spring arrives, the humpback whales migrate, many of them to the cool coastal waters off Alaska and northern Canada. There they find seas rich with the krill and small fish that sustain them. Mothers who have just given birth have been losing weight at the rate of a hundred pounds a day—or more—for months, and are now ready to feast. Though the humpbacks have no teeth, nature has given them an ingenious way to obtain food from the water, filtering it through balleen, a kind of screen that lets the water slip through while the food is trapped inside the whale's mouth. Whales feed throughout the summer, gaining weight and strength for their 3,000-mile journey back to tropical waters, where the females give birth, renewing the cycle. Most whales are born sometime between early December and mid-January. Calves nurse for the first year of their lives, gaining a remarkable five to seven pounds an hour as they do so. Their rapid weight gain gives calves a fighting chance of making the difficult journey north to the feeding grounds. Though the humpback is far from the largest living whale, some reach a weight of forty tons. That's fairly impressive for an animal that swims over 6,000 miles a year.

Sample B

Slack Guitar

Slack guitar has become increasingly popular in recent years even though the sound is not all that new, because it actually goes back as far as the 1800s, so it is now part of jazz, folk music, country, and it can even be heard in some classical music. The term "slack" comes from the fact that some of the strings on the guitar are slack, or loose, and so picking them creates a slightly different sound than picking taut strings, so then a player will sometimes pick the bass or rhythm on the lower strings and then pick the melody on the top because this creates a kind of haunting, twangy sound that many people like and then they will want to buy the music.

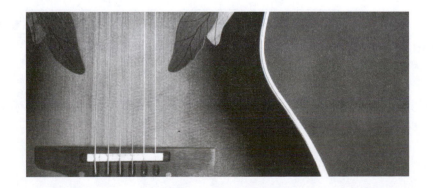

Revision of Sample B

Slack Guitar

Slack guitar has become increasingly popular in recent

years⊙ ~~even though~~ The sound is not all that new, ~~because~~ *dating back to*

but infused with modern music, it has revitalized

~~it actually goes back as far as~~ the 1800s, ~~so it is now part of~~

even

jazz, folk music, country, and ~~it can even be heard in~~ some

classical music. The term "slack" comes from the fact that

some of the strings on the guitar are slack, or loose⊙ ~~and~~

~~so~~ Picking them creates a slightly different sound than

What's more,

picking taut strings⊙ ~~so then~~ a player will sometimes

pick the bass or rhythm on the lower strings and then pick

The result is

the melody on the top⊙ ~~because this creates~~ a kind of

find irresistible—so much so that they feel compelled

haunting, twangy sound that many people ~~like and then~~

~~they will want~~ to buy the music.

Sample C: Whole Class Revision

Lightning

> and, but, so, because:
> Overused?
> Clear connections?
> Varied beginnings?

From the time of Benjamin Franklin with his famous kite experiment, and even for hundreds of years before that, people have been fascinated by lightning, and it is no wonder for it is not only beautiful to look at, but it can also be incredibly dangerous because the air immediately surrounding a bolt of lightning can be as hot as 18,000 degrees F, and the lightning bolt itself may be hot enough to fuse sand into glass. Lightning strikes throughout the world, but is most common in Central Africa, and even though it has been seen in virtually every state in the U. S., it is most common in the Midwest and Gulf states, and less common in Alaska and Hawaii. Even though no one knows *precisely* how lightning is formed, scientists are coming closer to explaining it, and it is believed that ice particles from inside clouds play a role, but lightning can also be triggered by the extreme heat of forest fires or even by volcanic dust.

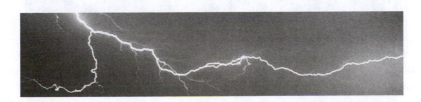

Sample D: Revising with Partners

**Shoplifting:
The Five-Finger Rip-Off**

and, but, so, because:
Overused?
Clear connections?
Varied beginnings?

Shoplifting is sometimes laughingly called the "five-finger discount," but there is really nothing so very funny about it from an economic standpoint because shoplifting costs American merchants millions of dollars daily and then in addition to that the real costs are passed along to the consumer in the form of price increases.

Most of the shoplifting done in the United States is done by amateurs and they may be people who cannot afford the merchandise, but sometimes they are people who get a supposed thrill from the shoplifting, but in addition, there are professional shoplifters and they can do real economic damage to retailers because they are highly skilled at what they do and can be more difficult to identify or capture, and that is one reason merchants value their customers' assistance in apprehending shoplifters.

Suggested Revisions of C and D

Sample C: Whole Class Revision

Lightning

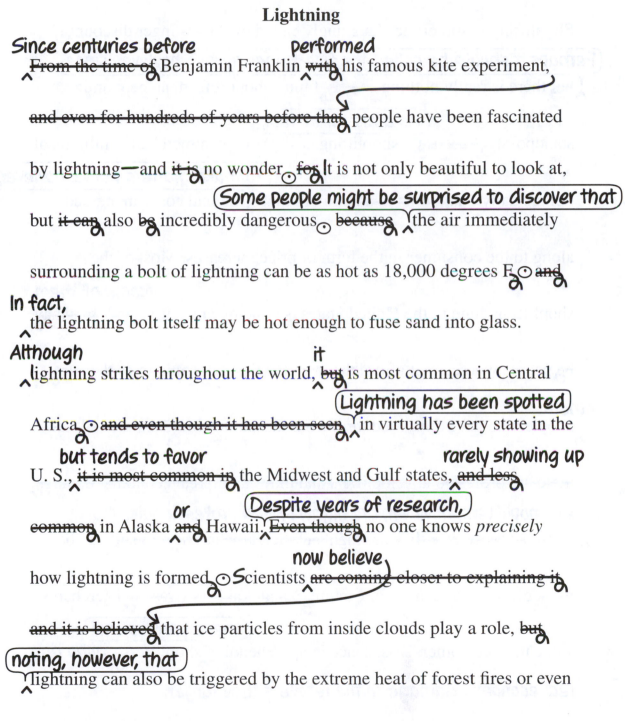

Since centuries before ~~From the time of~~ Benjamin Franklin performed ~~with~~ his famous kite experiment, ~~and even for hundreds of years before that~~ people have been fascinated by lightning—and ~~it is~~ no wonder. ~~for~~ It is not only beautiful to look at, Some people might be surprised to discover that but ~~it can~~ also ~~be~~ incredibly dangerous. ~~because~~ the air immediately surrounding a bolt of lightning can be as hot as 18,000 degrees F. ~~and~~ In fact, the lightning bolt itself may be hot enough to fuse sand into glass. Although lightning strikes throughout the world, ~~but~~ it is most common in Central Africa. ~~and even though it has been seen~~ Lightning has been spotted in virtually every state in the U.S., ~~it is most common in~~ but tends to favor the Midwest and Gulf states, ~~and less~~ rarely showing up ~~common~~ in Alaska ~~and~~ or Hawaii. ~~Even though~~ Despite years of research, no one knows *precisely* how lightning is formed. Scientists ~~are coming closer to explaining it~~ now believe ~~and it is believed~~ that ice particles from inside clouds play a role, ~~but~~ noting, however, that lightning can also be triggered by the extreme heat of forest fires or even by volcanic dust.

Sample D: Revising with Partners

Shoplifting: The Five-Finger Rip-Off

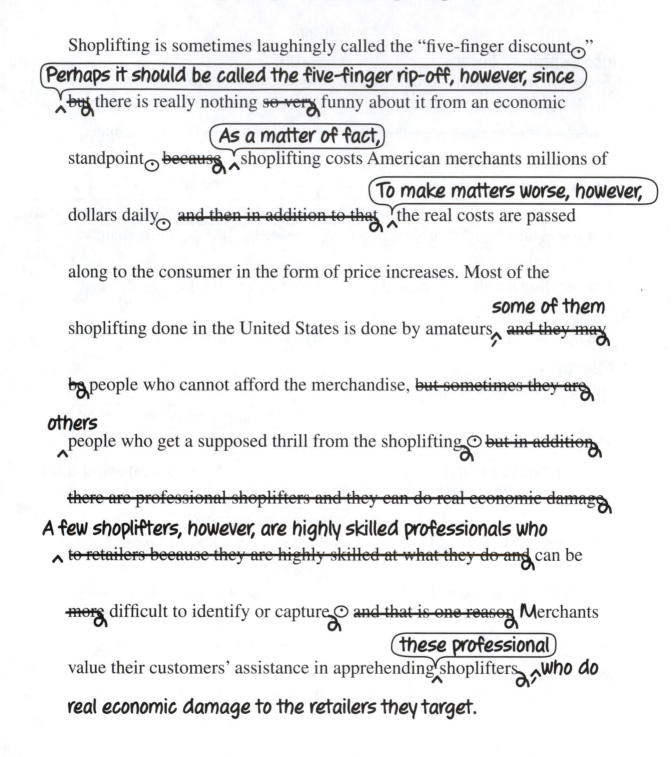

Shoplifting is sometimes laughingly called the "five-finger discount."
~~Perhaps it should be called the five-finger rip-off, however, since~~
~~but~~ there is really nothing ~~so very~~ funny about it from an economic

As a matter of fact,

standpoint. ~~because~~ shoplifting costs American merchants millions of

To make matters worse, however,

dollars daily. ~~and then in addition to that~~ the real costs are passed

along to the consumer in the form of price increases. Most of the

some of them

shoplifting done in the United States is done by amateurs, ~~and they may~~

be people who cannot afford the merchandise, ~~but sometimes they are~~

others

people who get a supposed thrill from the shoplifting. ~~but in addition~~

~~there are professional shoplifters and they can do real economic damage~~

A few shoplifters, however, are highly skilled professionals who

~~to retailers because they are highly skilled at what they do and~~ can be

~~more~~ difficult to identify or capture. ~~and that is one reason~~ Merchants

these professional

value their customers' assistance in apprehending shoplifters who do

real economic damage to the retailers they target.

The Small Stuff

Trait Connection: **Conventions**

Introduction (Share with students in your own words—or as a handout.)

Are you the sort of person who notices a misspelled word on the grocery marquee? Does it bug you when you run across a typo in a published book or newspaper? If so, this lesson is definitely one you'll enjoy. It's all about spotting small problems that are not likely to be caught by a computer spell checker—or through cursory editing. These are the kinds of errors you're especially likely to make if you write or type rapidly. And if you also *read* rapidly, you're unlikely to spot them later. How many errors can you spot in these examples?

- Over a hunderd thousand spetators showed up for the Ball game lost Friday.

- Once he swing the bat we new he was going tobe a home run

- It was for degrees celcius, but Im not sure how that converts to Fahrenhiet.

- The Census bureau calculate that he U.S population is rapdly approaching 300 million.

- In technical writing; most numbers are written asa figures.

- Its often customary to write out numbers such sixty thousand, that can be be expressed in too words.

- Helping the humans live in harmony with nature has the goal of the Natural Resources Defence Counsel.

If you found *at least* two errors per sentence, you are developing a good editor's eye. If you found more, you're a natural editor. If you did not find all the errors, here are some tips for editing carefully when it counts. First, read the sentence aloud. It will slow you down a little, and also help you hear things like repeated or missing words or missing punctuation. Second, use a ruler to mark the line you're currently reading. This keeps your quick reader's eye from skipping ahead. In addition, do not depend on your computer to catch errors. Computers help—and that's all. If a computer recognizes a word as legitimate—such as *to*—it does not always flag the word, even if you should have written *too*. Moreover, computer program rules governing grammar and punctuation may or may not match those in your handbook. Finally, when you write a draft, double space to make revising and editing easy. Later, read your draft both silently and aloud to look and listen for errors, pencil in hand, handbook at your side.

Teaching the Lesson (General Guidelines for Teachers)

1. Share the examples above, or make up your own examples to offer students practice in spotting the "little things."

2. Let them know that this lesson does not focus on any particular rules, but covers a wide range of *small* errors likely to show up in unedited or hastily edited text: missing or repeated words, misspellings, missing punctuation, faulty capitals, words run together, and so on.

3. Make sure students have access to a good handbook (*Write Source: The New Generation* published by Great Source Education is recommended) to which they can refer during the lesson.

4. Share the editing lesson on the following page. Ask students to read the text aloud, looking and listening for errors. It may be helpful for some students to use a ruler to mark lines of text as they go.

5. Ask students to edit individually first, then check with a partner.

6. When everyone is done, ask them to coach you as you edit the same copy.

7. When you finish, compare your edited copy with our suggested text on page 224.

Editing Goal: Catch as many small errors as possible (out of 35) through careful editing.
Follow-Up: Watch for small errors in your own work.

Answers to Warm-Up Sentences

- Over a hundred thousand spetators showed up for the Ball game last Friday.

- Once he swing the bat, we new he was going tobe a home run.

- It was for degrees celsius, but Im not sure how that converts to Fahrenhiet.

- The Census bureau calculate that he US population is rapdly approaching 300 million.

- In technical writing; most numbers are written as figures.

- Its often customary to write out numbers such sixty thousand, that can be be expressed in too words.

- Helping the humans live in harmony with nature has the goal of the Natural Resources Defence Counsel.

Editing Practice

Look for small errors.

Its facinating to watch behind the scenes as specialists bring movie to life. So many step are involved. For one thing, scouts must identify a suitable location: a a city, seascape, forest, dessert, or whatever. If te right location cannot be found (New York city in the 1840s, for example), it was to be built, often at grate cost. Researchers sit about to uncover the smallest details. What did people of the time wear? What did their hair look like? How did they talk? What sort off furniture did they have in there houses? Something as small what you see on te dining room table can make a film look authentic—or poorly researched. Actors must be coach too speak and walk and ever gesture in a way that fits 1880s Texas or or 1740s France. Luckly for directors and producers, special affects can creates background scenery (like whale boats pull into port or space ships landing in feilds), as well as explosions or transformations into alein creatures But even in a film about so-called "normal people—who run a book store, lets say—viewer's can besure that each book on the shelve is hand-0picked by someone. No wonder its cost so much to make films.

Edited Copy

35 errors corrected

Its facinating to watch behind the scenes as specialists bring movie to life.

So many step are involved. For one thing, scouts must identify a suitable

location: a a city, seascape, forest, dessert, or whatever. If te right location

cannot be found (New York city in the 1840s, for example), it was to be

built, often at grate cost. Researchers sit about to uncover the smallest

details. What did people of the time wear? What did their hair look like?

How did they talk? What sort off furniture did they have in there houses?

Something as small what you see on te dining room table can make a film

look authentic—or poorly researched. Actors must be coach too speak and

walk and ever gesture in a way that fits 1880s Texas or os 1740s France.

Luckly for directors and producers, special affects can create background

scenery (like whale boats pull into port or space ships landing in feilds), as

well as explosions or transformations into alein creatures But even in a film

about so-called "normal people—who run a book store, lets say—viewers

can besure that each book on the shelve is hand-picked by someone. No

wonder its cost so much to make films.

Revising the Set-Up

Trait Connection: **Sentence Fluency**

Introduction

Imagine for a moment that you are out somewhere having dinner, and a perfect stranger plunks him- or herself down at your table and begins to eat. You are likely to wonder who this intruder is, and what he or she is doing there. Readers have the same sort of response to a quotation that seems to fall out of the sky. It sounds more like an interruption than an integral piece of the writing. A well-chosen quotation can give your writing credibility—and voice. Quotations only work their magic, however, when they are set up effectively. To set up an interesting comment well, you might use words like *As Ramirez says, . . .* or *Lewis tells us that . . .* or *Arquette takes a similar position when she says, . . .* In this lesson, you'll have a chance to create a smooth set-up for each quotation so that it is welcomed into the conversation, not seated unexpectedly next to a very surprised reader.

Teacher's Sidebar . . .

Choosing the right quotation is the first step in providing strong support for informational or persuasive writing. It is not enough by itself, however. If a quotation is not set up properly, the reader may miss the point entirely. Student writers should be able to say of each quotation they select, "I am including this in my writing because _____." Whatever goes in that blank can then be used, in some form, to craft an introduction that helps readers know precisely what to look and listen for. Please note that all quotations in this lesson include citations. If the format does not match what is acceptable in your classroom, please use this opportunity to discuss proper format.

Focus and Intent

This lesson is intended to help students:

- Understand the importance of setting up a quotation well.
- Distinguish between quotations that are set up effectively and those that are not.
- Revise a passage by giving a "dropped from the sky" quotation the set-up it needs to give a passage informational or persuasive power.

Teaching the Lesson

Step 1: Creating a Set-Up

Each of the following passages includes a quotation. Though the passage may provide a small hint about why the writer is quoting someone else, the quotation is not set up effectively. Revise to create a set-up that links the quotation to the point the writer is trying to make. The first one is done for you.

1. Why did people in the early 1960s participate in the Freedom Rides? "The answer is simple. It was the right thing to do." (Jim Zwerg in *Freedom Riders* by Ann Bausum. 2006. Washington, DC: National Geographic Society, p. 6.)

Smoother Set-Up

Why did people in the early 1960s participate in the Freedom Rides? **Freedom Rider Jim Zwerg speaks for many people of his generation when he tells us,** "The answer is simple. It was the right thing to do." (Jim Zwerg in *Freedom Riders* by Ann Bausum. 2006. Washington, DC: National Geographic Society, p. 6.)

2. In *The House on Mango Street* by Sandra Cisneros, the speaker, Esperanza, shares her thoughts about life and her family. "Nenny is too young to be my friend. She's just my sister and that was not my fault. You don't pick your sisters, you just get them and sometimes they come like Nenny." (Sandra Cisneros, *The House on Mango Street*. 1984. New York: Random House, p. 8.)

Smoother Set-Up

_____

_____

3. Author Gary Paulsen wrote the book *Guts* to help readers understand the true-life adventures that formed the basis for *Hatchet* and other books about Brian. "So much of what I did as a boy came to be part of Brian—all of it in some ways. I hope that *Guts* satisfies those readers that want to know more about Brian and my life." (Gary Paulsen, *Guts*. 2001. New York: Random House, *Foreword*.)

Smoother Set-Up

_____

_____

Step 2: Making the Reading-Writing Connection

In his book *The Adventures of Marco Polo*, author Russell Freedman enlivens the text with many quotations from Polo's own book, *The Description of the World*. He also quotes other well-known figures of the 1200s. In doing so, he allows readers to see and hear the world through the eyes of people who lived during Marco

Polo's time, centuries ago. In the following passage, Freedman is describing the efforts of Polo's party to cross the Hindu Kush, braving steep trails at an elevation of 15,000 feet in their effort to reach the city of Kashgar, in what is now China. Notice how Freedman interweaves his own voice with that of Marco Polo:

Sample

"No birds fly here because of the height and the cold," Marco reported. He noticed that "fire does not burn so brightly, or give out as much heat as usual, and food does not cook as well." He believed that the weak flames were due to "this great cold." Actually, the flames were weak because of the oxygen-thin air at that altitude.

(From *The Adventures of Marco Polo* by Russell Freedman. 2006. New York: Scholastic, p. 21.)

Are there any jarring moments in this passage? Do you ever feel as if an unexpected guest is suddenly dropping in on you? Read the passage aloud, more than once, to appreciate just how smoothly Freedman weaves the two voices—his own and Polo's—together to create one message.

Step 3: Involving Students as Evaluators

Ask students to review Samples A and B, looking and listening for a smooth set-up for each quotation. Encourage students to work in teams, reading aloud and talking about whether each quotation sounds more like a smooth, integral part of the message—or an abrupt intrusion. Encourage them to make marginal notes about how any given quotation might be set up more effectively.

Discussing Results

Most students should find Sample A stronger. The writer takes care to set up each quotation effectively, showing just how it fits into the larger discussion and why it is important to the point he wishes to make. By contrast, writer B simply drops the quotations into the text, leaving it to the reader to decipher their significance. Talk about differences between the two pieces, and about how writer B might set up her quotations more effectively. One possible revision of Sample B is provided.

Step 4: Modeling Revision

- Share Sample C (*Whole Class Revision*) with students. Read it aloud.
- Ask whether this writer sets up quotations effectively, or simply drops them into the text. (Most students should say *drops them in.*)
- Read each quotation aloud, and discuss its importance. Why is the writer using it? What point does the quotation make or support?
- Read the sentence *preceding each quotation* aloud, slowly. Does that introduction make it clear who is speaking? Does it show precisely why the quotation that follows is important to the larger discussion?

■ Revise the current introduction, or add a new sentence to set the quotation up effectively. Feel free to add or cut anything to make the introduction read smoothly. (Invent details if you need to do so.)

■ Compare your draft with ours if you wish, keeping in mind that your revision need not match ours—so long as each quotation is set up effectively.

Step 5: Revising with Partners

Share Sample D (*Revising with Partners*). Ask students to follow the basic steps you modeled with Sample C. *Working with partners,* they should:

■ Read the passage aloud, looking and listening to see whether the writer has set up each quotation effectively.

■ Take time to discuss the quotations themselves. Why did the writer choose them? What point does he or she wish to make?

■ Take time to read the sentence introducing each quotation. Does that introduction make it clear who is speaking, and why that voice should be part of the larger conversation?

■ Revise by adding any information that will set up each quotation effectively.

■ Read their revisions aloud to hear the impact of their changes.

■ Compare their revisions with ours, keeping in mind that their revisions need not match ours.

Step 6: Sharing and Discussing Results

When students have finished, ask several pairs of students to share their revised passages aloud. How many different ways did teams find to set up quotations effectively? Do you have favorites? If so, make a poster to which you can refer as you work on informational or persuasive pieces.

Next Steps

■ Pull any lively quotation—at random—from a newspaper or current periodical. Brainstorm as many ways as you can to introduce the quotation. Imagine that it will appear in an informational piece on the same general topic as the article from which you pulled it.

■ If your students are currently working on a research-based piece, ask them to review their own writing, focusing on the words they have used to introduce each quotation. Ask them to make sure each one is set up as a smooth, integral part of a larger conversation.

■ Newspaper articles focusing on political or social issues almost always include quotations—sometimes from people with opposing points of view.

Pull several, and examine the set-ups the journalists have used. Did they present each quotation well? Could it have been done better? Ask students whether they would be satisfied with the introduction if they were one of the persons being quoted.

■ *For an additional challenge:* What makes for a good introduction to any quotation depends a little on the source of the quotation. For a challenge, ask students to draft an informational piece that includes quotations from an encyclopedia, reference book, journal or periodical, and live personal interview. Talk about which sources come closest to capturing the human voice—and how this in turn influences the way in which a quotation is set up.

Sample A

| Effective set-up? |
| or |
| Sudden drop-in? |

Monster: In the Eye of the Beholder

People who have not read Mary Shelley's book *Frankenstein* are unlikely to appreciate just how articulate Dr. Frankenstein's monster actually was. True enough, the monster was depicted as hideous in appearance, but many people also picture him as rude, bumbling, and incoherent—and that is far from the case. The movies have done much to influence the way we see this creature. Films based on Shelley's book have been made about once a decade since the industry began, but the most well-known is the 1931 classic starring Boris Karloff. In that film, says writer and visual arts specialist Karen Karbiener, "the creature's huge, square head, oversized frame, and undersized suit jacket still inform most people's idea of what Shelley's monster 'really' looks like" (xvi). But, there is more to the monster than a lurching physical presence. In contrast to the 1931 interpretation, Karbiener points to the 1994 film *Mary Shelley's Frankenstein,* in which actor Robert DeNiro "did not wear the conventional face paint and restored the monster's eloquent powers of speech" (xvi). This interpretation, Karbiener adds, gave the monster a new "emotional range" (xvii), and may even influence how some film goers read Shelley's book—as it enjoys renewed popularity.

Source: **Karen Karbiener,** *Introduction* to *Frankenstein* by Mary Shelley. 2003. New York: Barnes and Noble Books.

Sample B

Moose Mania

Effective set-up?
or
Sudden drop-in?

In the book *Guts*, author Gary Paulsen writes of several encounters with moose in the wild. "I just saw brown. I saw big. I saw death coming at me, snorting and thundering" (p. 35).

During one particularly memorable—and odd—encounter, the moose pays very little attention to Gary at all. "It looked no different than other small pine trees, cute and well formed, like a little Christmas tree, but in that bull's mind maybe the tree had done something to insult him, or gotten in his way or called him out, because he absolutely destroyed that tree" (p. 36).

These encounters provided the background that enabled Paulsen to make the moose attacks on Brian, in the book *Hatchet*, seem so realistic.

Source: Gary Paulsen, *Guts*. 2001. New York: Random House.

Revision of Sample B

Moose Mania

In the book *Guts*, author Gary Paulsen writes of several encounters with

During one attack, he barely has time to react. He describes it this way:

moose in the wild. "I just saw brown. I saw big. I saw death coming at

me, snorting and thundering" (p. 35).

another

During ~~one~~ particularly memorable—and odd—encounter, the

Instead, it directs all its rage toward a small tree. As Gary explains,

moose pays very little attention to Gary at all. "It looked no different

than other small pine trees, cute and well formed, like a little Christmas

tree, but in that bull's mind maybe the tree had done something to insult

him, or gotten in his way or called him out, because he absolutely

destroyed that tree" (p. 36).

helped Paulsen understand how maniacal moose can be, and

These encounters provided the background that enabled ~~Paulsen to~~

him to

make the moose attacks on Brian, in the book *Hatchet*, seem so realistic.

Sample C: Whole Class Revision

Safer in Today's Traffic

> Effective set-up?
> or
> Sudden drop-in?

Though there are roughly ten times as many cars on the road today as there were in 1930, it turns out that driving may actually be safer. There are many reasons for this, according to *Wall Street Journal* reporter Cynthia Crossen. "Early cars had weak brakes, tires that blew out, headlights that glared, plate-glass windows that shattered . . . no seat belts, and often soft roofs or no roofs at all" (p. B1). Pretty much anyone who wanted to drive could drive. "There were no drivers' education requirements, no driving exams, no vision tests, no age limits" (p. B1). "In most places, there were no speed limits" (B1).

"Pedestrians also played a part in the mayhem. They crossed in the middle of blocks, popped out from between parked cars and tried to 'beat' the car bearing down on them" (B1). No wonder that even with so many more cars on the road, the percentage of drivers involved in accidents has actually declined dramatically.

Source: Cynthia Crossen. "Unsafe at Any Speed, With Any Driver, On Any Kind of Road." *Wall Street Journal*. Vol. CCLI, No. 51. New York: March 3, 2008. Page B1.

Sample D: Revising with Partners

Effective set-up?
or
Sudden drop-in?

The Challenge of Memoir

Award winning author and historian Jennifer Armstrong helped hero Irene Gut Opdyke write the biographical account of Opdyke's role as a resistance fighter during the Holocaust. Though Opdyke lost her home and family to the Nazis, she fought back, helping Jews escape to freedom, and spying on the SS, at great risk to her own life. Armstrong did considerable research to prepare for the book, and also interviewed Opdyke personally. "I prepared approximately thirty pages of questions to ask Irene, and when I went to meet her, we spent a week talking about her experiences" (p. 9).

Armstrong wrote several historical novels before taking on Irene's story. "In some ways it's harder to write Irene's story. Real life doesn't necessarily conform to the rules of narrative" (p. 9). It was difficult from Opdyke's perspective, too. "You can't always recall every conversation you had, or the name of every street you walked on, or every person you met over fifty years ago when you were in fear for your life," Armstrong says (p. 6).

Source: Jennifer Armstrong in "A Reader's Guide." From Irene Gut Opdyke with Jennifer Armstrong, *In My Hands: Memories of a Holocaust Rescuer*. 1999. New York: Random House.

Suggested Revisions of C and D

Sample C: Whole Class Revision

Safer in Today's Traffic

Though there are roughly ten times as many cars on the road today as there were in 1930, it turns out that driving may actually be safer. ~~There are many reasons for this.~~ According to *Wall Street Journal* reporter **there are many reasons for this, including problems with older cars:** Cynthia Crossen, "Early cars had weak brakes, tires that blew out, headlights that glared, plate-glass windows that shattered . . . no seat **That's not the whole story, though. In those days,** belts, and often soft roofs or no roofs at all" (p. B1). Pretty much anyone **whether they were qualified or not, because as Crossen tells us,** who wanted to drive could drive. "There were no drivers' education requirements, no driving exams, no vision tests, no age limits" (p. B1). **Crossen adds that** "In most places, there were no speed limits" **either** (B1).

Crossen explains. "Pedestrians also played a part in the mayhem," ~~They crossed in~~ **She points out that they typically "crossed in** the middle of blocks, popped out from between parked cars and tried to 'beat' the car bearing down on them" (B1). No wonder that even with so many more cars on the road, the percentage of drivers involved in accidents has actually declined dramatically.

Source: Cynthia Crossen. "Unsafe at Any Speed, With Any Driver, On Any Kind of Road." *Wall Street Journal.* Vol. CCLI, No. 51. New York: March 3, 2008. Page B1.

Sample D: Revising with Partners

The Challenge of Memoir

Award winning author and historian Jennifer Armstrong helped hero

Irene Gut Opdyke write the biographical account of Opdyke's role as a

resistance fighter during the Holocaust. Though Opdyke lost her home

and family to the Nazis, she fought back, helping Jews escape to

freedom, and spying on the SS, at great risk to her own life. Armstrong

did considerable research to prepare for the book, and also interviewed

a task that Armstrong says took both time and planning:

Opdyke personally, "I prepared approximately thirty pages of questions

to ask Irene, and when I went to meet her, we spent a week talking about

her experiences" (p. 9).

Armstrong wrote several historical novels before taking on Irene's

but found the genre of memoir to be even more of a challenge.

story, "In some ways it's harder to write Irene's story. Real life doesn't

a challenge

necessarily conform to the rules of narrative" (p. 9). It was ~~difficult~~ from

because while accuracy is important, Armstrong explains that

Opdyke's perspective, ~~too~~, "You can't always recall every conversation

you had, or the name of every street you walked on, or every person you

met over fifty years ago when you were in fear for your life." ~~Armstrong~~

~~says~~ (p. 6).

Source: Jennifer Armstrong in "A Reader's Guide." From Irene Gut Opdyke with
Jennifer Armstrong, *In My Hands: Memories of a Holocaust Rescuer.* 1999. New
York: Random House.

Presentation

Trait Connection: **Conventions**

Introduction (Share with students in your own words—or as a handout.)

There's an old saying almost everyone has heard: *Don't judge a book by its cover.* There may be plenty of wisdom embedded in those words as they apply metaphorically to *people*, but when it comes to books themselves, covers matter—quite a lot. A good book cover may make the difference in whether you pick the book up in the first place. Book covers are an outstanding example of presentation: how information is presented on the page. Notice not only the cover but the inside page of a textbook or novel, the front page of any newspaper, a brochure or poster, a menu, greeting card, or advertisement, and you'll be looking at the result of dozens, sometimes hundreds, of little decisions about how to make information look good, how to make it accessible, and how to get the attention of someone like *you*, the reader.

For what we might call "everyday writing," meaning narratives, informational research pieces, persuasive essays, and so forth, presentation deals mostly with such issues as font style and size, margin size, headings and subheadings, graphics, and footnotes or endnotes. These decisions are still important, though. They influence the readability and general appeal of your document. Let's say you're a design editor receiving one of your own documents to be published. Can you answer the following questions?

1. What font will you use?

2. What *size* font will you recommend for the basic text? What size paper?

3. How big will your margins be?

4. Will your document be double spaced, single spaced, or something else?

5. Will you use *italics*, **boldfaced** print, or <u>underlining</u> for emphasis?

6. Will you number pages? Upper right, lower right, or alternating right and left?

7. Will you have headings (titles and subtitles)? If so, will they appear in the same font—or a different font from the rest of your text?

8. Will you center them on the page—or place them differently?

9. Will you need to cite sources? If so, will you use footnotes (each page) or endnotes (at the end of your document)? What format will you follow?

10. Will you use bulleted or numbered lists?

11. Will you have graphics? Photos? Charts? Cartoons?

12. Will anything appear in color? If so, how *many* colors?

If you can answer these questions, you have just *begun* to think about a few of the issues that design editors deal with each day. Pay attention to the printed documents in your life, and even though you may not have the technology to imitate everything you see, you'll gather a wealth of ideas you can use to give your own documents eye appeal—and ensure that readers can quickly, easily find what they're looking for.

In the lesson that follows, you'll have a chance to do a critique of the design and layout of one page. With a partner, you'll consider as many issues as occur to you, imagining that you could re-do the design completely. There are no rights or wrongs here. This is about making information look good on the page.

Teaching the Lesson (General Guidelines for Teachers)

1. Share the list of 12 presentation questions, encouraging students to think through how they would design one of their own documents if they had the technology and resources to make *any decisions they wished.* You may want to take some time for this discussion. (Their answers will depend, in part, on whether they have computer access, and what programs are available to them. Take some time to discuss this, too.)

2. To expand this part of the lesson, consider looking at covers and front matter for several different books. Also compare front pages of major newspapers, such as the *Wall Street Journal*, the *New York Times*, and *USA Today*. Talk about differences and what your students find appealing—or any changes they would like to see. If you have other documents available (menus, brochures, etc.), you may wish to include those also.

3. Take time to discuss how presentation fits within your own curriculum. What issues are most important (or less important) for the kinds of documents your students will produce in your classroom? In what circumstances might other issues become important? (Think résumés, graduation announcements, business letters, etc.)

4. Remind students that this lesson focuses not on rules but on what is most (1) appealing to the eye, and (2) helpful to a reader seeking specific information. With respect to point 2, for example, a list can be buried within the text, or made to stand out with numbers or bullets. Key points can be emphasized with subheads (or at least paragraphs) or blended together in one large body of text.

5. Share the editing lesson on the following page. Ask students to read the text aloud, thinking about how the information could be more effectively orga-

nized. Ask them to think of as many ideas for making this piece visually striking as they can—and with their partners, to make a list.

6. When everyone is done, invite students to join in a class discussion of possibilities, and if you wish, make a class list of design recommendations.

7. When you finish, compare your list with our suggested revision. (Note that the original is written in Ifficina Sans Bold 11 point text. Revised text is Helvetica Neue 12-point, with heads done in Marker Felt Thin 26-point (main head) and 18-point (subheads).)

Editing Goal: Think about issues of design.
Follow-Up: Do whatever is practical and possible to make your own documents visually appealing and readable. If possible, scan the editing practice copy into your computer and give students a chance to revise it online.

Editing Practice

Consider visual presentation.
List possible design revisions.

Many famous people have suffered from headaches, including Sigmund Freud, author

Virginia Woolf, director Frank Capra, and playwright George Bernard Shaw. While

frequently occurring, long lasting headaches may be signs of a more serious

condition, most headaches are of relatively short duration, and stem from such

everyday factors as lack of sleep, tension, exposure to prolonged bright light, food

allergies, eye strain, or inflammation. These self-limiting headaches are usually

treatable, and sufferers report success with a range of remedies. Perhaps the most

common way to treat a headache is with aspirin or other painkiller, but other

potential treatments include increased sleep, meditation, avoidance of loud noise or

bright light, massage of neck and shoulder muscles, and avoidance of foods known to

trigger allergic reactions. Some people even report that stroking a cat or dog helps—

but as yet, there is little scientific evidence for this unorthodox remedy.

Design Suggestions:

Re-Designed Copy

Headaches
Causes

Many famous people have suffered from headaches, including Sigmund Freud, author Virginia Woolf, director Frank Capra, and playwright George Bernard Shaw. While frequently occurring, long lasting headaches may be signs of a more serious condition, *most* headaches are of relatively short duration, and stem from such everyday factors as

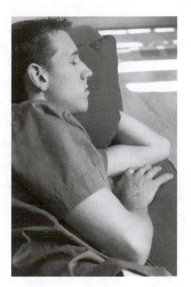

- lack of sleep,
- tension,
- exposure to prolonged bright light,
- food allergies,
- eye strain, or
- inflammation.

These self-limiting headaches are *usually* treatable, and sufferers report success with a range of remedies.

Treatments

Perhaps the most common way to treat a headache is with aspirin or other painkiller, but other potential treatments include

- increased sleep,
- meditation,
- avoidance of loud noise or bright light,
- massage of neck and shoulder muscles, and
- avoidance of foods known to trigger allergic reactions.

Some people even report that stroking a cat or dog helps—but as yet, there is little scientific evidence for this unorthodox remedy.

Revising with Multiple Strategies

Trait Connection: **Sentence Fluency**

Introduction

Many things go into making sentences fluent and readable. You likely know some strategies for creating fluent writing—but perhaps you have not tried applying them all at one time. In this lesson, you'll have a chance to use at least four: eliminating *There is* or *There are* beginnings; putting the emphasis on the end note; combining sentences to smooth the flow; and using transitional expressions (*After a while, On the other hand, For example*) to link ideas. Perhaps this seems like a lot to keep in mind. Remember, though, these small strategies all connect to one larger purpose: making the flow of ideas both fluent and easy to follow.

Teacher's Sidebar . . .

Students sometimes begin a "multiple strategy" approach by trying to use *every* strategy with *every* sentence. This quickly becomes both confusing and overwhelming. A better technique is to read a piece aloud, sometimes more than once, looking for opportunities to improve the flow or logic of the sentences. A student writer may wind up using one strategy several times within a piece, and another not at all. Also, student writers may find themselves making one or two changes on the first pass, then reading aloud and making one or two more. Avoid a formulaic approach. Instead, simply remember that a piece is "revised" for fluency when it reads smoothly.

Focus and Intent

This lesson is intended to help students:

- Recall several strategies for improving fluency.
- Distinguish between fluent and non-fluent writing.
- Revise a passage by applying one or more strategies to increase sentence flow and readability.

Teaching the Lesson

Step 1: Taking the Fluency "Crash Course"

Following are some suggested strategies for improving fluency. Apply each one in turn—and feel free to do a second revision if you can improve the sentence further. Add any words or details you need. Feel free to invent, as if the writing were your own. In each case, one example is done for you.

Strategy 1: Avoid weak *There is, There are* sentence openings.
1. There are many reasons to engage in high school sports.

   High school students who participate in sports enjoy many benefits.

2. There is reason to believe that stress impairs test performance.

   _____

Strategy 2: Put the most important point *last* in the sentence.
1. Jason was fired when his employer discovered he was seeking another job.

   When his employer discovered he was seeking another job, Jason was fired.

2. Ruth Ann screamed and the dog dove right through the window when a large black shadow appeared.

   _____

Strategy 3: Combine closely related sentences to improve the flow.
1. Often it rained. It rained especially hard in the spring. Then the swamps would fill to overflowing. That brought in great flocks of wild geese.

   It rained especially hard in the spring, filling the swamps to overflowing and bringing in great flocks of wild geese.

2. To some extent, unemployment is seasonal. It tends to decline during the summer. At that time, part-time positions open up in recreational industries.

   _____

Strategy 4: Use a transitional expression to show connections.
1. Everyone in Rebecca's family wanted her to attend the wedding. She decided not to go.

   Even though everyone in Rebecca's family wanted her to attend the wedding, she decided not to go.

2. Olympic athletes make gymnastics look easy. It is very difficult.

   _____

Step 2: Making the Reading-Writing Connection

In *Who Was First? Discovering the Americas*, Russell Freedman re-examines the "discovery" of the Americas, revealing fascinating information about people who significantly pre-dated Columbus as explorers—and inhabitants—of both continents. Notice the careful crafting of sentences in this passage from the chapter titled "Who Really Discovered America?"

Sample

First they found a skeleton: the ancient bones of a giant woolly mammoth buried in a dried-up lake bed near Clovis, New Mexico.

Then, as archaeologists uncovered the mammoth's bones, they spotted a lethal Stone Age weapon. Lying next to the skeleton was a large stone spearhead. Evidently, the mammoth had been killed by hunters hurling a spear with the sharp stone point attached to its tip.

(*Who Was First? Discovering the Americas* by Russell Freedman. 2007. Boston: Houghton Mifflin, p. 71.)

Look carefully at Freedman's sentence beginnings. Do they seem purposeful to you? Do they tie his ideas together and make the text easy to follow in the reader's mind? Try starting one or more sentences with *There was* or *There were*. Notice the effect this has on fluency. Now look at each sentence ending. Does Freedman save the most important point for last—or would you flip any of these sentences around? Notice how many individual ideas are embedded in Freedman's first and last sentences. If you were to break either one down into tiny sentences (one idea per sentence, no more), how many would you need to create? Try it and see. On a scale of 1 to 6, how high do you think Freedman would score on the trait of sentence fluency? (To truly appreciate his skill, read more.)

Step 3: Involving Students as Evaluators

Ask students to review Samples A and B, looking and listening for fluency—or for passages that could be revised using one or more of the four fluency strategies discussed in this lesson. Encourage students to work in teams, with highlighters in their hands, marking any troublesome passages and making marginal notes about revision possibilities.

Discussing Results

Most students should find Sample B stronger. The writer avoids weak beginnings, links ideas together well, and combines several related ideas in one sentence. In addition, important points tend to come last in the sentence, giving them additional emphasis. By contrast, writer A favors weaker beginnings and ignores opportunities to link ideas through transitional expressions. Some sentences could be flipped to put the most important point at the end—where it receives rhythmic emphasis. One possible revision of Sample A is provided.

Step 4: Modeling Revision

- Share Sample C (*Whole Class Revision*) with students. Read it aloud.

- Ask whether this writer uses strong sentence beginnings, effective transitions, emphatic sentence endings, and strategic combining to avoid numerous choppy sentences. (Most students should say *no*.)

- Give students time to review and discuss the passage in teams.

- As a class, identify opportunities for revision, and discuss the best ways of improving the text.

- With students' guidance, make any revisions you wish, using the four strategies discussed in this lesson together with any ideas of your own.

- Feel free to flip sentences, cut anything, or add new words or phrases so that the piece reads smoothly. When you finish, check the effectiveness of your revision by reading it aloud. (*Note:* It is sometimes helpful for students to listen as you read, but *not follow along visually*. Revised text can be visually distracting when a reader is trying to listen for fluency.)

- Compare your draft with ours if you wish, keeping in mind that your revision need not match ours—so long as you improved the fluency.

Step 5: Revising with Partners

Share Sample D (*Revising with Partners*). Ask students to follow the basic steps you modeled with Sample C. *Working with partners,* they should:

- Read the passage aloud, looking and listening for opportunities to improve the fluency.

- Discuss the passage together, highlighting problems and/or making marginal notes.

- Use the four strategies from the lesson—and any other ideas—to make revisions, focusing on fluency and reading aloud as they test their revisions.

- Read the final revision aloud with one person *just listening*—not following along visually. Make any additional revisions.

- Compare their revisions with ours, keeping in mind that their revisions need not match ours.

Step 6: Sharing and Discussing Results

When students have finished, ask several pairs of students to share their revised passages aloud. Do they sound very different? How many different strategies did teams use to improve fluency?

Next Steps

- Choose sentences at random from any textbook your students are currently using. Revise each sentence as many ways as possible within 90 seconds, doing the revisions as a competition with teams. Which team can come up with the most fluent revision?

- Ask students to review their own writing, looking for opportunities to apply the four strategies identified in this lesson. Ask volunteers to read "before" and "after" versions aloud to the class.

- Watch and listen for carefully crafted sentences in the literature you share aloud. Listen especially for sentences with strong beginnings and endings. Recommended:

  - *Who Was First? Discovering the Americas* by Russell Freedman. 2007. Boston: Houghton Mifflin.

  - *Escape! The Story of the Great Houdini* by Sid Fleischman. 2006. New York: HarperCollins.

  - *Living Up the Street* by Gary Soto. 1985. New York: Bantam Doubleday Dell.

  - *No More Dead Dogs* by Gordon Korman. 2000. New York: Hyperion.

  - *Team Moon: How 400,000 People Landed Apollo 11 on the Moon* by Catherine Thimmesh. 2006. Boston: Houghton Mifflin.

- *For an additional challenge:* Invite students needing a challenge to create a lesson by taking any well-written passage of 50 to 100 words (from a published work—check our list of recommended books) and "revising it" by introducing three or more of the four fluency problems discussed in this lesson. They can then trade with each other or present the lesson to the class. See how many problems revisers working to improve the passage can find—and correct. Read the final drafts aloud and compare them to the published originals, remembering that good revisers sometimes improve upon published work!

Sample A

There is, There are?
Transitions?
Combined ideas?
Important point at
the end?

Great Waffles

There is no perfect waffle recipe, but just about everyone thinks he or she has the best one! Most waffles made in the U.S. today contain yeast. This makes the waffles rise. It also makes them fluffy. There were actually waffles in the Middle Ages, too. They did not contain yeast, however. They were more like crispy cakes, and were sometimes shaped into cones. Some had the family coat of arms embedded right on the waffle. Many people eat waffles with maple syrup. There are other ways to enjoy waffles, though. Peanut butter makes a good topping. Jam or fresh fruit are good, too. There are even some people who like waffles with chicken. There are probably as many waffle toppings as there are waffle lovers, and they include chocolate, sour cream, whipped cream, ice cream, and honey. Then there are so-called "healthy" waffles made from ingredients like oats, flax, seeds, and various whole grain flours. Why not enjoy a waffle for breakfast tomorrow?

Sample B

There is, There are?
Transitions?
Combined ideas?
Important point at
the end?

Irish Folk Dancing

Irish dancing has become increasingly popular in recent years. It has a long tradition, dating back to pre-Christian times in Ireland. Some sources say it began with sailors, dancing on the decks of ships to entertain themselves during long months at sea. Because they often had little space in which to move, they learned to keep the dance confined. Originally, the steps followed a kind of free spirited style, but over the years, traditions evolved. For example, unlike other forms of dance, Irish dance calls for the dancer to keep the upper body, especially arms and hands, relatively still. This can be a challenge when one's feet are moving rapidly—and even more so when the dancer is kicking his or her legs very high! In addition, it is often customary to follow steps with both feet: whatever the left foot does, the right must do also. As anyone who has observed Irish dancers can testify, it is also part of the tradition to tap the feet solidly against the dance "floor," creating a rhythmic beat. The speed with which dancers' feet move, the dancers' incredible balance and control, and the rhythm of shoes tapping against floorboards all work together to give Irish dancers and their audience an exhilarating experience.

Revision of Sample A

Great Waffles

Maybe you think you have the
There is no perfect waffle recipe. but just about everyone thinks he or
If yours is like most modern American recipes, it contains
she has the best one! Most waffles made in the U.S. today contain yeast
to make   and give   a   texture.
This makes the waffles rise. It also makes them fluffy. There were
actually Waffles in the Middle Ages, too. They did not contain yeast,
but instead
however. They were more like crispy cakes, and were sometimes shaped
and often having
into cones. Some had the family coat of arms embedded right on the

Today's waffle toppings are as varied as waffle lovers.
Depending on how adventurous you are, try them with
waffle. Many people eat waffles with maple syrup. There are other ways
to enjoy waffles, though. Peanut butter makes a good topping. Jam or
—or even
fresh fruit are good, too. There are even some people who like waffles
               Waffle lovers with a real sweet tooth might want to pile on
with chicken! There are probably as many waffle toppings as there are
                                                                 the
waffle lovers, and they include chocolate, sour cream, whipped cream,
               Or, go the other direction, and use
ice cream, and honey. Then there are so-called "healthy" waffles made
from ingredients like oats, flax, seeds, and various whole grain flours
to create a delicious but "healthy" waffle.
No matter what kind of waffle lover you are,
Why not enjoy a waffle for breakfast tomorrow? Feeling Medieval? Go
ahead—carve your initials into the top!

You'd be far from alone!

Sample C: Whole Class Revision

Falconry

During the Middle Ages, falconry, or hawking, was a popular sport. Falconry was practical because it brought meat to the table. In those days, many people lived mainly on bread. There were not many people who could afford falcons. They were expensive. There was a certain nobility and prestige involved in owning and using falcons. Also, it took time to train them. Falconers would sing to their birds. They would also stroke them with feathers. There was certain gear a falcon would wear. This included a hood to keep the falcon quiet until it was time to go after the prey. There was also a leash that kept the bird tethered to a perch until it was released. The falcons used in hunting were almost always females. This is because the female birds of prey were larger. They were able to go after larger prey. There were severe penalties for stealing a falcon during the Middle Ages. A thief could be imprisoned—or worse. It was sometimes hard to settle disputes. A person who caught a falcon might argue that the bird belonged to him. But the person who owned the land usually claimed ownership of any falcons captured there.

Sample D: Revising with Partners

Coyotes

> There is, There are?
> Transitions?
> Combined ideas?
> Important point at
> the end?

Coyotes can be found throughout Central and North America from Panama north to Alaska. There are many subspecies of coyote. They tend to look alike, however. The coyote is the size of a fairly large dog. It is smaller than a wolf, however. Coyotes sometimes mate with dogs. Their pups called "coydogs" can be dangerous. They hunt like coyotes. They are also aggressive. But like dogs, they are not afraid of humans. This makes them dangerous. There is almost nothing the coyote will not eat. This is why the coyote is successful even in areas where their hunting grounds have been taken over by humans. Coyotes like fresh meat best. They will kill rabbits, squirrels, and other rodents to get it. They will even kill young or injured livestock. But if there is no meat available, they will eat vegetables. Garbage works, too. There are almost no instances in which coyotes have attacked humans. It is not unheard of, however. A hungry coyote will pursue a biker or a child. It will also kill small pets. There is reason to believe the coyote will be around forever because it is so adaptable.

Suggested Revisions of C and D

Sample C: Whole Class Revision

Falconry

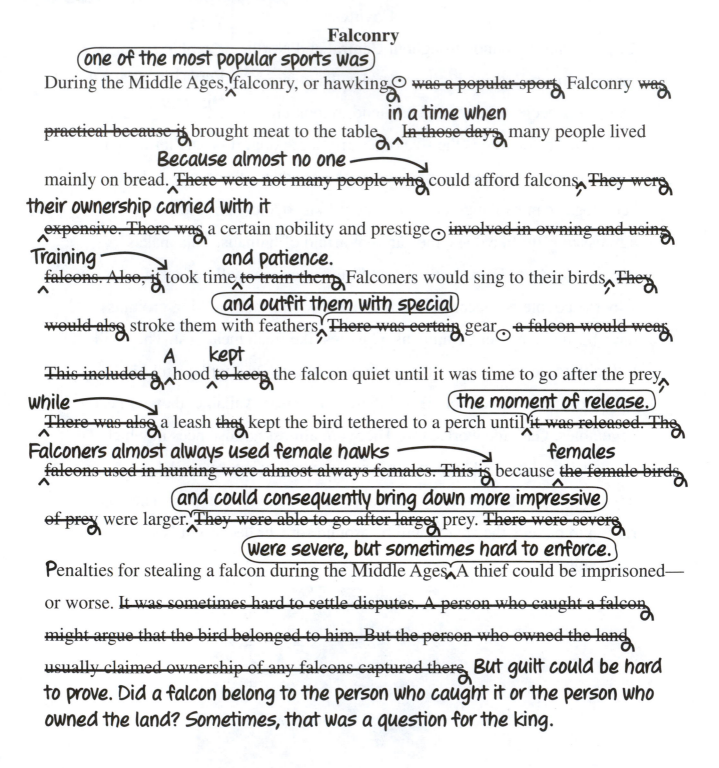

During the Middle Ages, falconry, or hawking ⊙ ~~was a popular sport.~~ [one of the most popular sports was] Falconry ~~was~~

~~practical because it~~ brought meat to the table. ~~In those days,~~ [in a time when] many people lived

mainly on bread. ~~There were not many people who~~ [Because almost no one] could afford falcons. ~~They were~~

~~expensive.~~ There was a certain nobility and prestige ⊙ ~~involved in owning and using~~ [their ownership carried with it]

~~falcons. Also, it~~ took time ~~to train them.~~ [Training and patience.] Falconers would sing to their birds. ~~They~~

~~would also~~ stroke them with feathers. ~~There was certain~~ gear ⊙ [and outfit them with special] ~~a falcon would wear.~~

~~This included a~~ [A] hood ~~to keep~~ [kept] the falcon quiet until it was time to go after the prey.

~~There was also~~ [while] a leash ~~that~~ kept the bird tethered to a perch until ~~it was released. The~~ [the moment of release.]

~~falcons used in hunting were almost always females.~~ [Falconers almost always used female hawks] This is because ~~the female birds~~ [females]

~~of prey~~ were larger. ~~They were able to go after larger~~ prey. ~~There were severe~~ [and could consequently bring down more impressive]

Penalties for stealing a falcon during the Middle Ages. [were severe, but sometimes hard to enforce.] A thief could be imprisoned—

or worse. ~~It was sometimes hard to settle disputes. A person who caught a falcon~~

~~might argue that the bird belonged to him. But the person who owned the land~~

~~usually claimed ownership of any falcons captured there.~~ But guilt could be hard

to prove. Did a falcon belong to the person who caught it or the person who

owned the land? Sometimes, that was a question for the king.

Sample D: Revising with Partners

Coyotes

Look almost anywhere

~~Coyotes can be found~~ throughout Central and North America from Panama north to

and you're likely to spot tracks of the crafty, omnipresent coyote.   *are almost indistinguishable. Most are about*

Alaska. ~~There are many~~ Subspecies of coyote. ~~They tend to look alike, however. The~~

but considerably   *which they otherwise resemble.*

~~coyote~~ is the size of a fairly large dog. ~~It is~~ smaller than a wolf, ~~however~~ Coyotes

producing dangerous, aggressive   *that*

sometimes mate with dogs. ~~Their~~ pups called "coydogs" ~~can be dangerous. They~~ hunt

but, like dogs, have no fear of

like coyotes. ~~They are also aggressive. But like dogs, they are not afraid of~~ humans.

Unlike dogs, coyotes will eat nearly anything, animal or vegetable, alive or dead.

~~This makes them dangerous. There is almost nothing the coyote will not eat. This is~~

No wonder that

~~why the coyote is successful~~ even in areas where their hunting grounds have been

they thrive. Though they're far from picky, they   *To get it, they*

taken over by humans. ~~Coyotes~~ like fresh meat best. ~~They~~ will kill rabbits, squirrels,

or

and other rodents ~~to get it. They will~~ even ~~kill~~ young or injured livestock. But if ~~there~~

is   *coyotes resort to*   *from the garden or yesterday's*

~~is~~ no meat available, ~~they will eat~~ vegetables, garbage. ~~works, too. There are almost~~

Though coyote attacks on humans are almost

~~no instances in which coyotes have attacked humans. It is not~~ unheard of, ~~however~~ a

Given the opportunity,

hungry coyote will pursue a biker or a child. It will also kill small pets. ~~There is~~

Love them or hate them, coyotes are so adaptable, they are likely destined to

~~reason to believe the coyote will~~ be around forever. ~~because it is so adaptable~~

Editing Wrap-Up
(All Editing Lessons for Grade 7)

Trait Connection: **Conventions**

Introduction (Share with students in your own words.)

In this lesson, you will have a chance to practice editing for errors and problems covered in all previous editing lessons. An editing checklist is provided to remind you what to look for.

Teaching the Lesson (General Guidelines for Teachers)

1. Share copies of the editing checklist (page 256) with students if you have not done so previously. Review anything that they do not recall. You may wish to laminate it or insert it into a plastic protective cover so students can mark it with a dry erase marker.

2. Make sure that students have access to a student handbook that reflects conventional rules applied in your classroom.

3. Remind students that this is not a test. It is a personal assessment, a chance for them to see how many conventional rules and suggestions they can recall and apply. (**Suggestion:** If you wish to test students' knowledge of conventions, use this lesson as a warm-up, and then have them (as soon as possible following the lesson) edit a piece of their own work. Base your assessment on the quality of the final draft combined with the degree of change from rough to final.)

4. Share the editing lesson on the next page.

5. Students should read the passage aloud *(softly)*, looking *and listening* for errors or problems. Please note that much internal punctuation is missing. Students will need to read carefully to distinguish sentences and clauses. In addition, they can mark new paragraphs using this symbol:¶ Once students have finished editing, ask them to think about presentation, and to be prepared to offer at least *three suggestions* for improvement.

6. Ask them to edit individually first, then check with a partner.

7. When everyone is done, ask them to coach you as you edit the same copy, making any changes you and they identify. Use carets, inverted carets, and delete symbols to make your corrections. Circle new periods.

8. When you finish, read your edited copy aloud to make sure you caught *everything*, pausing to discuss your editorial changes. Also discuss suggestions for improving the presentation, considering both (1) eye appeal, and (2) accessibility of information. Compare your version to our suggested copy on page 259.

9. If students have any difficulty, review as necessary and repeat this lesson, asking students to work with different partners.

**Editing Goal: Correct 45 errors. Re-design the presentation.
Follow-Up: Look for editorial changes needed in your own work.
Consider presentation as appropriate.**

Editing Checklist

___ **Carets** (^) used to insert words or corrections

___ **Delete symbol** (ℰ) used to take things out

___ **Semicolons** used to link short, related sentences (independent clauses): *We had liver for dinner; Betty ate out.*

___ **Semicolons** used to separate elements in a complex series (elements already containing commas): *Brian's new semester schedule included Latin, which was far from his favorite subject, though he excelled at it; chemistry, which gave him a chance to do the outrageous experiments he loved; and ecology, which was a brand new course, and the one Brian was most excited about.*

___ **Colons** used to set up words, phrases, or whole sentences: *Else had but one goal: winning. Team members held their breath as the coach made his call: "out of bounds." Over and over the thought echoed in his mind: Stealing is wrong.*

___ Jarring **shifts in tense** corrected:
From—I **was riding** my bike along the sidewalk when a dog **runs** right in front of me.
To—I **was riding** my bike along the sidewalk when a dog **ran** right in front of me.

___ Jarring **shifts in person** corrected:
From—**I** don't like exploring caves because **you** feel so closed in.
To—**I** don't like exploring caves because **I** feel so closed in.

___ Sentences revised in formal writing to **avoid casual use of *I* or *you***:
From—**You** can't describe the thrill America experienced when Apollo 11 landed on the moon.
To—**All of America** was thrilled when Apollo 11 landed on the moon.

___ **Modifiers put in place** to avoid ambiguity: *From*—She took off with her boyfriend throwing an angry glance back at us. *(Who was angry?)*
To—Throwing an angry glance back at us, she took off with her boyfriend.

___ **Capitals used** where needed: Ike graduated from Yale University.

___ **Capitals avoided** where *not* needed:
From: Arlene spotted a Bobcat in the Wilderness.
To: Arlene spotted a bobcat in the wilderness.

___ Careful editing to catch **little things**: missing or repeated words and letters, missing punctuation, words run together, misspellings, etc.

___ Review of **presentation** to be sure it is pleasing to the eye and directs readers' attention to key information

___ *Everything* read both silently AND aloud, pencil in hand, handbook nearby

> *Author's Note:* Please remember that this editing checklist is designed for use with these Grade 7 lessons, and is *not meant to be comprehensive*. For a review of numerous other conventional issues, I invite you to explore editing lessons (and corresponding Editing Checklists) for other grade levels in the *Creating Revisers and Editors* series.

Editing Practice

Correct any errors you find. Make 3 or more recommendations for effective presentation.

Fore young people who enjoy travel but find it to expensive, heres a possible solution employment on a Cruise Ship. Positions are available for Chiefs who may work in a cafeteria setting or specialize in delicacies like Sushi Health and Recreation Directors who coach travelers what want to keep fit while on vacation an various types of Assistants who handle everything from greeting guests and processing paperwork to cordinating laundry pickup. Work is intense, but benefits are generous. Pay is good. addition, many people found they get more free time than they expected. One caution, though it is important for applicants not get seasick easily. Morover, you must be comfortable confined in small spaces—sometime without windows. Guests get the rooms directly on the ocean staff get inside offices and sleeping quarters. But here the good news A person who finds all this appealing can go everwhere from antartica to Greenland, with te most popular destinations being cities on the Meditarranean, the Behamas, Mexico, Austrailia, and central America. Perhaps the Industry's new Motto should be "Get paid to travel!"

Edited Copy

45 errors corrected

For young people who enjoy travel but find it to expensive, heres a possible solution employment on a cruise ship. Positions are available for chiefs who may work in a cafeteria setting or specialize in delicacies like sushi health and recreation directors who coach travelers what want to keep fit while on vacation an various types of assistants who handle everything from greeting guests and processing paperwork to cordinating laundry pickup. ¶Work is intense, but benefits are generous. Pay is good. addition, many people found they get more free time than they expected. ¶One caution, though it is important for applicants not get seasick easily. Morover, you must be comfortable confined in small spaces—sometime without windows. Guests get the rooms directly on the ocean staff get inside offices and sleeping quarters. ¶But here the good news A person who finds all this appealing can go everwhere from antartica to Greenland, with te most popular destinations being cities on the Mediterranean, the Bahamas, Mexico, Australia, and central America. Perhaps the industry's new motto should be "Get paid to travel!"

Edited Copy (as it would appear in print)

Get Paid to Travel!

For young people who enjoy travel but find it too expensive, here's a possible solution: employment on a cruise ship. Positions are available for chefs, who may work in a cafeteria setting or specialize in delicacies like sushi; health and recreation directors, who coach travelers that want to keep fit while on vacation; and various types of assistants, who handle everything from greeting guests and processing paperwork to coordinating laundry pickup.

Work is intense, but benefits are generous. Pay is good. In addition, many people find they get more free time than they expected.

One caution, though: It is important for applicants not to get seasick easily. Moreover, applicants must be comfortable confined in small spaces—sometimes without windows. Guests get the rooms directly on the ocean; staff get inside offices and sleeping quarters.

But here's the good news: A person who finds all this appealing can go everywhere from Antarctica to Greenland, with the most popular destinations being cities on the Mediterranean, the Bahamas, Mexico, Australia, and Central America. Perhaps the industry's new motto should be "Get paid to travel!"

Note on Presentation: We divided the copy into four paragraphs, with paragraphs single spaced, and double spacing between. We added a heading, set in 36-point Marker Felt Thin. The body of the text has been changed from Times 14-point to Helvetica 12-point. The graphic of the cruise ship is woven into the text. A page border has been added.